# HOW TO THRIVE AND SURVIVE IN YOUR CLASSROOM

MARJAN GLAVAC
and
PAUL JACKSON

Publisher Data & Legal Information

© 2019 Marjan Glavac and Paul Jackson

Title: How to Thrive and Survive in Your Classroom

Format: Paperback

This publication has been assigned: 978-1-9991631-3-6

Title: How to Thrive and Survive in Your Classroom

Format: Electronic book

This publication has been assigned: 978-1-9991631-5-0

For free resources for getting a teaching job, becoming an effective teacher and making teaching fun, visit:

www.TheBusyEducator.com

# TABLE OF CONTENTS

# BUILDING THE FOUNDATION FOR THRIVING

## Introduction

### Teaching Tenets

These tenets are offered by Paul Jackson and Marjan Glavac as food for thought. Here are some tenets we believe are important for successful teachers.

**Definition:**  principles or doctrines held in common by members of a group; a set of beliefs common to the group.

Examples:

Work smarter, not harder!

Kaizen—practice the philosophy of continuous improvement.

The Serenity Prayer—

God grant me the serenity

To accept the things I cannot change,

Courage to change the things I can,

And wisdom to know the difference.

Teamwork is important.

Minimalize Instruction—Maximize Expectations (teach less, expect more).

Chunking makes learning easier—breaking the large into smaller, more manageable parts.

Teachable moments—be aware of them and don't feel guilty about using them.

Transfer is important and should be practiced by the teacher and taught to students.

Be "realistic"—use time for reflection to define your reality.

Quality of input = quality of output!

Do what works!

Quality over quantity is generally the best choice.

You are responsible for you! Teach that to your students as well.

Visuals work better than words.

Less talk (yours) is better than more talk.

Don't reinvent the wheel—beg, borrow, and steal ideas. There is really nothing original in teaching.

It's all about growth and what we become, not what we acquire.

Change is more important than outcome.

Work backwards with the end in mind. *This is a life skill.*

Take baby steps to teach students.

Avoid the negative nay-sayers on staff. Seek out the "like-minded".

Never, never, never give up!

Change is painful; teaching is change and it isn't easy.

80% of discipline problems can be solved by changing the environment.

Actions speak louder than words—talk less and take action more often.

You need to believe in yourself if you want students to believe in themselves.

You can only do one thing at a time.

It's okay to say *No*. In fact, you should deliberately practice it. Prepare your 'no' responses in advance so you are ready when the request comes.

It's okay to fail, apologize, and ask students for feedback; this allows students to help you!

Fill up your buckets first BEFORE filling up your students' buckets (take care of yourself—as often as you can).

Don't beat yourself up for mistakes—no one's perfect.

Don't complain about the things you can't do anything about.

Pick your battles (pick your hill to die on).

Take an advocate roll for your students. Sometimes you may be the only advocate she/he has.

Remember—whatever you do MAKES a difference in the lives of your students.

YOU are the most important influence in your students' lives in that classroom.

Teachers are like farmers—they plant seeds; seeds that sometimes take decades to grow and mature.

Appreciate the "control" you have of the environment in the classroom.

Every child has something good to share, a strength—it's your job to find it and nurture it.

Just because it worked last year, doesn't necessarily mean it'll work this year—every year's class is different!

## "Wisdomisms" or Truisms about Teaching

Marjan Glavac and Paul Jackson offer these for your professional reflection.

Examples:

Never do more than is absolutely necessary to meet the requirements of the legislated curriculum UNLESS the payback is very worthwhile.

Leverage as much as possible—ask your students, parents, and fellow teachers for help! Don't reinvent the wheel…

No one will thank you for putting out 150% effort, especially when 100% should have been plenty! Are you working harder than you really need to?

Don't beat yourself up and try to be perfect—do your best, but don't stress yourself out doing it!

The individual student is more important than the class in terms of your impact on them. Get to know as much as you can about your students as individuals

Impart to students that the only true measure of understanding is doing something that demonstrates that understanding (i.e. tests, assignments, projects, questions and answers, reports, demonstrations).

Take time for reflection and personal/professional development. This applies equally well to students. Teachers should model and students should learn about reflection as a personal/professional development tool.

Have students write "What I learned today" in their Victory or Learning Logs before the end of each day. Not a bad idea for the teacher as well!

Classroom teachers have more control of what goes on in their classrooms than they think they do. Use that to your advantage.

Progress is more important than the goal, especially if it is arbitrarily expected.

Focus your teaching on the majority and deal with the minority on a needs basis.

In terms of behavior, the best interests of the class in general take precedence over the behavior of the individual. Don't sacrifice the majority for the minority.

Teach the absolute minimum curriculum objectives for each unit of study using the time you have available. Once the minimum has been taught, use the remaining allotted time for enrichment for all the students.

Everything in life has to be prioritized. Recognize this and practice it. You cannot do everything.

You must give yourself permission to "not" do something; do something that you know will work, and do what is right.

You can only control the present moment; whatever you decide to do, you're deciding not to do something else.

If you add something to your curriculum, you must take something away. If you add another responsibility, you must remove a responsibility or delegate that responsibility.

Connect your teaching to real-world situations and current events. This changes the focus to how students can make a difference, not why they should make a difference. It gives the application for the knowledge and a reason to learn.

Use project-based learning. This provides "realistic situations" where the attitudes, skills, and knowledge a student needs has a purpose and a context in which the learning is meaningful.

Connect your teaching to what students already know and what they are interested in.

Teachers need to be respected, not liked or loved! Love and like are bonuses.

You're not their friend—you're their teacher.

Assessment and evaluation should be up front with students. Do this—get this! Use rubrics and targets in your assessment. Give out the "test" or grading system at the start of the assignment.

Tell students what the goals of the lesson/unit are; get feedback after each lesson/unit on whether the goal was met and how it could be improved. Keep detailed notes for the next time you teach the unit.

A.S.K.—

There are only three things you can teach and three things you can learn!

**A**ttitudes

**S**kills

**K**nowledge

Attitudes require reflection and direction, leading to action plans, goals, and objectives.

Skills come from knowledge and require DOING something—applied knowledge.

Knowledge is easy to get—books, Internet, peers, training, education, etc.

Attitudes are the most important of the three things we can teach and learn.

Your attitude determines your altitude!

# Reflection as a Personal and Professional Development Activity

*Paul Jackson*

## Reflection

In order to create a kind of vision of an ideal classroom or an ideal school or an ideal educational system, you must first take the time to REFLECT.

*The vision you create based on this reflection provides the framework within which every decision you make regarding the classroom, school, system…moves you one step close to your IDEAL!*

**"Thinking is the hardest work there is which, is the probable reason why so few people engage in it".**
*—Henry Ford*

## The Visionary Process

| | | |
|---|---|---|
| **REFLECTION** | *Head* | |
| *PAST* | | |
| **WRITING** | *Hand* | |
| *PRESENT* | | |
| **VISION** | *Heart* | |
| *FUTURE* | | |

# THREE TYPES OF REFLECTION

| REFLECTION ON ACTION | = | is a reflection on **past** practices, actions and thoughts | 1. How do I feel about the situation?<br>2. What went well?<br>3. What did not go as well as I expected?<br>4. What options did I consider as I selected my behaviour-actions?<br>5. What option did I choose?<br>6. How did I know what I chose to do was the best at the time and on what did I base that decision?<br>7. How did I know that another behaviour-action would not be appropriate?<br>8. What made this situation unusual?<br>9. What might I have done differently? 5. |
| REFLECTION IN ACTION | = | is a reflection in the **present** on practices, actions and thoughts while in the midst of | 1. What cues from the person or group do I see that tell me how they are responding to my behaviour-actions?<br>2. What assumptions or inferences am I making?<br>3. What options are available? What are the possible consequences of each? What would work best in this situation?<br>4. What principles-theories are guiding me?<br>5. What is unique about this situation?<br>6. What level of direction-specificity-structure is best here? 5. |
| REFLECTION FOR ACTION | = | is a reflection for the **future** combining the reflecting ON and the reflecting IN actions indicating what **will** happen. | 1. What did I learn that I can apply in other situations?<br>2. How did I alter my knowledge, theories, or attitudes as a result of this experience?<br>3. What did I learn from this situation that confirms my intuition?<br>4. What will I remember from the situation?<br>5. If I were in a similar situation again, how would I behave? 5. |

*"Reflective practice engages the teacher (principal-educator) in a cycle of thought and action based on professional experience portraying the teacher more as a creative artist-designer than as engineer-technician."*

*—Bud Wellington*

## REFLECTION AS A PROFESSIONAL DEVELOPMENT ACTIVITY

The following notes are based on article by Joellen Killion, Guy Todnem, Bud Wellington, and Cindy Harrison, as referred to in the bibliography.

**REFLECTION What's the big deal? Doesn't everyone do it?**

Consider these thoughts on reflection—

**Reflection is** a rich source of continued **personal and professional growth.**

Busy people typically do not engage in formal reflection. They rarely **treat themselves** to reflective experiences **unless** they are **given some time**, some **structure**, and the **expectations to do so.**

Reflection requires two things: **conscious metacognitive processing**…and **time** to reflect.

As professionals…**reflection is a gift** we give ourselves… with rigor…with purpose…and in some formal way, so as **to reveal the wisdom embedded in our experience.**

Establishing **routines** to make time **for reflection, using** trusted **colleagues** as sounding boards, and keeping **journals** are all helpful. **Reflection is more productive when guided by a process.**

Reflective practice engages the teacher in a **cycle of thought and action** based on professional experience.

Through reflection, we **develop context-specific theories** that **further our own understanding** of our work and **generate knowledge to inform future practice.**

# THE GREEN-YELLOW-RED REFLECTION PROCESS

*Paul Jackson*

## The Traffic Light Approach to Analysis

### Basic Premise

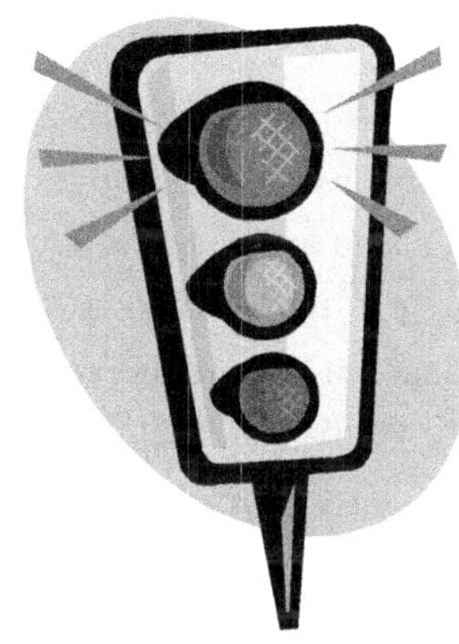

Using the three primary colors of green, yellow, and red, and a magic marker, highlighter, or Crayola marker…you can quickly analyze a document or list of ideas using color to give a visual clue of the overall picture after the reflective analysis.

Typically the traffic lights have red on top, yellow in the middle, and green on the bottom. Consider the horizontal stop lights found in some states of the United States with the red on the left, yellow in the center, and green on the right.

### How It Would Work

Using highlighters or erasable markers (Crayola) and the three colours—green, yellow, and red—you would make reflective judgments about the items in your list or parts of a document.

# GREEN

Green would indicate that the item being reviewed was a **"keeper"** that should be left unchanged and included in the document or list. This item is important and should be retained.

Notes **could** be made as to how to "tweak" the item to make it even better, but little or no change would be required.

# GREEN = GO

### *Taking the traffic light analogy even further*

A green light means you can proceed, but be aware that danger could lurk just ahead or around the corner. You are never totally safe on green, but it is a great place to be. Green carries you forward, but the green light doesn't last forever. You must constantly be aware that it could turn to yellow or even red if you don't pay attention to it.

Flashing green lights indicate that it is alright to keep going but there may be dangers imminent, since oncoming traffic could be a problem when turning left; or then again, a flashing green light might give you the right of way to keep going as long as it is safe to do so.

Green lights with arrows indicate a direction you should be going and that you are safe to do that. Green is a directional color. Green gives you the go-ahead to start new things and carry on with things the way they are according to the rules.

# YELLOW

Yellow would indicate the item being reviewed as in need of some "**change**". The basic value of this item is good. Major changes may be required and a different approach to it might be necessary, but the basic premise for inclusion on the list or in the document is still sound.

Notes **should** be made as to what changes would be required to make this item more acceptable under the present circumstances.

## YELLOW = CAUTION (Change is Coming)

*Taking the traffic light analogy even further*

The light is about to turn red. This is a warning of imminent danger and you should slow down because trouble is ahead. Don't suddenly speed up because you want to "ignore" the signal.

It is unsafe to proceed under yellow (caution). You must be aware of what it is that places you in this caution position. Stop what you are doing unless you wish to get into trouble.

Yellow means you can proceed with caution with no need to stop, but it could be dangerous if you don't accept the fact that it is yellow.

# RED

Red would indicate that the item being reviewed would have to be "**removed or replaced**". Think of all the "red" words that start with "r"—removed, replaced, reinvented, revamped, rewritten, rejuvenated, relegated to the trash bin…these red items are no longer relevant, out-of-date, not applicable anymore, flawed in principle, irrelevant to today's situation, and beyond saving! These are the items that must be removed permanently, replaced with entirely new version, or will require the creation of entirely new item.

Notes **must** be made as to what the replacement should be like and what should be included in this new item.

# RED = STOP

**You must create a new "green" now or remove the item altogether!!!**

*Taking the traffic light analogy even further*

It is common in most jurisdictions that you can make a right turn on a red light. This is what "red" items need—a major change in direction! You must stop first and realize that it is a red item, then when the way is clear and your plans are made, you can make a major change in direction.

Flashing red lights are warning devices. A major change is coming, but only after you have come to a complete stop and realized that major changes are required. Flashing red lights at intersections and railroad crossings or on school buses tell you there is imminent danger and you must not proceed.

Seeing "red" in this situation is a good thing. You recognize the problems and set goals to eliminate those problems.

**Additional Examples in the Traffic Light Analogy**

1. If the traffic lights aren't working, you are in trouble. It is truly a time for stopping first, analyzing the situation, then proceeding with caution.

2. Taking a shortcut at a red light through a conveniently located gas station or business parking lot is against the law. Shortcuts to success are usually fraught with danger and the consequences can be disastrous in terms of money lost and reputation ruined.

3. U-turns, in some situations, are a disaster and illegal as well as dangerous, but in other situations a U-turn might be exactly what you need. If done properly with extreme caution and adequate planning, U-turns can be very successful.

**Examples of where this reflective analysis could be used:**

1. If you are analyzing a plan (e.g. business plan) or document (e.g. a policy statement), you would read through the plan and after reflection, discussion, and analysis, you would decide whether or not each of the items in the plan would warrant a green, yellow, or red rating. The summative response would be clearly visible by the colors on the document.

2. If you are analyzing a list of items such as the steps in a process (e.g. a sales and marketing process) or a checklist for quality control, you would decide whether or not each item was relevant, useful, or meeting the objectives of the list by placing a green, yellow, or red rating on it. The summative response would be clearly visible by the colors on the document.

My personal pledge to me from me in order to begin the change process —

# WITHIN

# THE NEXT

# 24 HOURS

# I

# WILL <u>BEGIN</u>

# THE CHANGE

# PROCESS

# BY...

# The PIC Triangle of Influence Philosophy for Permanent Change

*Paul Jackson*

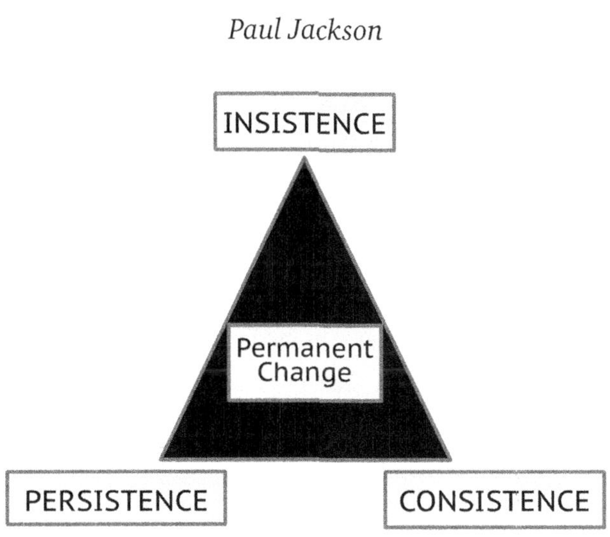


## How influential are you?

As an educational leader in a classroom, school, or a system, you are often faced with the dilemma of whether or not your influence as a leader is affecting others. The PIC Philosophy of Permanent Change is an attempt to give an individual a framework within which to work. Every decision you make can then be influenced by this philosophical point of view. There are many ways to arrive at the same destination, but the ultimate goal of a leader is to have his/her influence felt permanently in change. In other words, what kind of influence do you have on everything that happens in your classroom, school, or school system?

The further removed a leader is from the most important people in the system, the more important it is that the leader feels that his/her efforts are being felt where it counts the most.

In the educational system, the bottom line is the students. That is where the leader's influence must be felt. In most instances, it is the influence of the teachers that is most important in order to impact the students. You must not only believe this is happening, but believe that is truly what your job is all about. For the school principal, this is indeed the case. The vast majority of principals aspired to that position with the intent on having more influence on the students or on the system in order to improve learning for students. If this is not the case, it should have been!

## Educational Leaders

Using educational leaders, as an example, there are many individuals besides the school administrator who are leaders in the educational system. Teachers are leaders in the classroom, school, and system. Parents are leaders in the school through Parent Councils. Students lead other students and influence teachers. Superintendents lead school administrators, politicians, and school board personnel. The philosophy can be applied in many educational and non-educational situations.

Let's look at this philosophy in terms of a school administrator, the staff, and the students. It could be applied in a similar manner to other organizational situations.

**P**ersistence

**I**nsistence

**C**onsistence

These three nouns describe the "necessities" for permanent change to take place. You can also use the "action" verb form of the words—Persistent, Insistent, Consistent.

Whenever something new is introduced which is designed to become a permanent change in an individual or a group, three leader traits must be exhibited in order to be effective.

If you are a parent, classroom teacher, instructor, supervisor, or any person whose job it is to make permanent changes in behavior, you must understand how the PIC philosophy summarizes what needs to be done.

## What does the triangle represent?

The vertices of the triangle represent the three traits required of the leader—persistence, insistence, and consistence. All three of these traits must be equally balanced in order for success to be achieved. The change agent—the leader—must exhibit these traits throughout the process.

Persistence is the ability of the leader to continue to "doggedly" continue with the actions necessary in order make the change come about. This also includes the continued introduction of new learning experiences to facilitate the change. The change is constantly kept in the minds of those who must change. The leader makes this change a priority and keeps it a priority. Resolve is communicated to the individuals who must change their behavior. The pressure to change is not going to go away.

There are no other options but to implement the changes. The target has been set and nothing less than success is acceptable.

Insistence is the ability of the leader to convince the individual or group that requires a change in behavior of the necessity of the specific goal to be accomplished. The new behavior must occur. Sometimes this is established by the needs of the group or individual. Sometimes it is a legal or moral or ethical obligation. Once the goal of change is established, it can't be altered. A good leader uses facts to establish the necessity of the change. The rationale must be explained and accepted by the person or group for whom the change is a necessity. The fact that there is no doubt that this change must occur is the insistence aspect of the change process.

Consistence is the ability of the leader to maintain, under duress, the enforcement of the change. The message will always be the same—the change will occur and you will change in order to reach the established goals. When rules or procedures are established, a leader will enforce them as a method of making sure the change takes place. There can be no exceptions to the established rules. The same message must consistently be delivered. Even when changes in procedure are implemented, the final end product must be delivered and any consequences must occur naturally as a part of the process.

So...

**Persistence = Doggedness**

**Insistence = Necessity**

**Consistence = Enforcement**

Let's take a look an example of how this would work in a typical school setting. As the administrative leader in the school, the principal is told by the board that a new reporting system and report card is to be implemented for the following school year.

In this situation, the **PERSISTENCE** aspect of the triangle of influence is enacted when a plan is established to gradually provide the required training for the implementation process. There will also be timelines and specific dates established in order to reach the goal by the designated time. Communication of the expectations for individuals or groups must be done so there is no confusion as to what is to be expected of everyone involved in the process. The leader will also communicate what he/she will do in order to facilitate the introduction of the change. The staff should be involved in the actual establishment of the plan to reach the goal. Consider the skills, knowledge, and attitudes that will need to be addressed in order to accomplish the task.

The **INSISTENCE** component of the triangle of influence for change is clearly of a "legislated" edict by the school board or regional political group in charge of the school system. The principal must still present the required change in behavior in such a manner that it will be accepted as a necessity, if not wholeheartedly endorsed. There can be no individual opting out of the required change in behavior, but there may be some flexibility in terms of implementation of the required changes.

Enforcement of the established timelines and activities that the staff must embark upon is the **CONSISTENCE** part of the triangle of influence. There cannot be a perceived special treatment for an individual or a relaxation on the insistence of the action plan being carried out. There must be consequences for an individual's inability or refusal to do what is required of him/her. When the time comes, everyone will be ready to implement the change and do it well. In other words, the new report cards will be used when they are required to be used and the teachers will do a good job of it, with help provided to everyone to accomplish the goal.

For the classroom teacher, any behavior you wish to change is subject to the PIC Philosophy of Change.

# LEARNING TO WISDOM-TRANSITION

**Step 1:**

**INFORMATION + EXPERIENCE = KNOWLEDGE**

This is learning.

***Knowledge is applied information*** *+ experience.*

**Step 2:**

**KNOWLEDGE + EXPERIENCE + REFLECTION = WISDOM**

Wisdom takes time and is born out of reflection.

**Wisdom is applied knowledge + experience + reflection.**

"Without reflection, experience is not cumulative"
—*Paul Jackson*

"Knowledge becomes wisdom only after
it has been put to practical use".
—*Paul Jackson*

**WISDOM SHOULD BE SHARED**

# Goals Begin Behavior –
# Consequences Maintain Behavior

**According to a Toronto Star newspaper survey on education:**

"...the ideal teacher is a person who actually teaches, who acts like a human being, and who tries to look attractive."

"Teacher Excellence: A Public Perspective". *Ontario Institute for Studies in Education*. Volume 19, No. 4. December 1988.

# THE A.S.K. PHILOSPHY OF TEACHING AND LEARNING

OR

## THE JUST ASK! PHILOSOPHY

*Paul Jackson*

What do you need to learn?
What do you need to teach?

**Just ASK!**

A personal philosophy of what we need to teach and learn.

There are only three things you need to consider when teaching something or learning something. These three things are summed up in the acronym ASK.

**A**ttitudes

**S**kills

**K**nowledge

all three need to be considered
every time you teach something
*and*
all three need to be assessed after the teaching.

This is an attempt to simplify the rather complicated curriculum documents we are charged with teaching into three very fundamental ways of looking at what we teach and what we learn.

Incorporating A.S.K. in all lessons ensures a successful teaching and learning experience.

## ATTITUDES

Attitude is the area of teaching and learning that gets the least amount of attention. It may arguably be the most important aspect, since attitudes shape an individual's behavior and each individual's attitude determines our collective identities.

The attitudes referred to here are of the broadest persuasion.

Attitudes are the 'mindful' part of all of our experiences.

They include such things as:

Beliefs

Postures

Positions

Tenets

Points of view

Stances

Values

Morals

Ethics

Feelings

Presumptions

Convictions

Principles

Impressions

Faiths

Assumptions

You get the idea. These are things that motivate us to behave in certain ways in given situations. They are the attitudes that shape our behavior, and it is behavior that makes us who we are.

**"Informal" teachers** in our society include parents, leaders, coaches, mentors, spokespersons, and friends where the teaching isn't considered the same as the formal part of teaching and learning in institutions. These people are still "teachers".

**In the "formal" teaching and learning situation** of schooling, the teachers may also be educators, instructors, and trainers. This A.S.K. philosophical statement deals primarily with this group of formal teachers, but can also apply to those informal teachers as well.

There is a reluctance to include the teaching of attitude in the curriculum because it is more difficult to teach and more difficult to measure than skills and knowledge. That is not a legitimate reason to avoid it. Most curriculum documents include attitudes in their objectives under various other names—values, beliefs, morals, and ethics being some of them.

In everything you teach, attitudes must be a prime consideration. Teachers influence the perceptions, judgements, attitudes, suppositions, and prejudices of their students whether they consciously attempt to or not. What's important is that teachers see attitudes as a legitimate and primary focus of all teaching and learning.

No summative assessment instrument used with students should be without an opportunity to express opinion, debate viewpoints, put things in perspective, argue a case, take a stance, or put the present reality in context with the historical background. Making a statement after learning something new makes the learning relevant to the learner. It's an opportunity for each individual to note where they started with their attitude and how it has changed or been reinforced. It is the affective component of learning. It's an imperative. It shapes the future.

Learners should be given the opportunity to express their attitudes <u>before</u> teaching takes place and an opportunity to express it again <u>after</u> new learning takes place. It is not a quantitative assessment but a qualitative expression of present attitudes. If "grading" the expression of attitudes is necessary, then consider the use of the knowledge and skills the learner uses to provide a rationale for his/her opinions. It's not easy doing this kind of assessment, but it can be done and should be done by all teachers.

The primary message here is that "Attitudes" should be a primary consideration in everything you teach and everything your students learn.

## SKILLS

Skills are distinguishable primarily because they can be used to do something and because all of us are capable of learning new skills or honing present ones to make the changes we desire.

Skills are the doing part of learning.

The difficulty often is we don't focus enough on teaching the skills of learning when it comes to knowledge acquisition. Take the example of a learner being given the assignment of preparing for and taking part in a debate. Having knowledge, information, or data to use in the debate isn't of much use unless the skills of researching and debating aren't learned at the same time in order to acquire the knowledge or put the knowledge to use. Skills are required to collect knowledge, learn the material, and use the acquired knowledge.

Teach skills. Never assume a learner already has the necessary skills at his/her disposal. Too often this assumption leads to frustration on the part of the learner when given a task for which he/she is unprepared to tackle. Practice the skills required of the learner. Emphasize skills over knowledge acquisition. Acquired skills make knowledge acquisition available to the leaner when the need arises. Skills provide the learner with a "life-long" access to knowledge.

Assess the skills not just the knowledge when testing for comprehension and mastery of new material. Expect a learner to demonstrate the newly acquired skills as part of the assessment. We are more than well aware that knowledge and data are readily available on the Internet for answers to any problem.

But if the search skills of using this resource aren't learned, then the Internet becomes as obstacle to learning, not an asset.

Knowledge is constantly changing and at a very rapid pace. The skills a learner acquires allows that learner to be in charge of his/her learning of new knowledge. Skilful people are successful people. Skills are a valuable commodity in the marketplace.

Perhaps it's not too difficult to believe that our individual "uniqueness" is distinguished more by the skills we possess than by the knowledge we have.

## KNOWLEDGE

Knowledge is the most recognizable of the three types of things we can teach and learn. It's the aspect that everyone wants to measure to prove learning took place. Knowledge is only one of the three components of teaching and learning.

Knowledge is best described as the "what" that you learn. It includes facts, information, data, and theories. It is the raw material of skills acquisition and usage. Knowledge is the "stuff" teachers are supposed to teach.

Knowledge is useless unless put to use.

The learner's attitudes and skills very much affect how knowledge will be used or whether new knowledge needs to be acquired. It is these same attitudes and skills that create new knowledge in order to solve problems.

"Knowing" something isn't of much use without the application of the knowledge. Far too much time is spent teaching knowledge out of context or with no purpose. True knowledge is acquired through doing something.

The assessment of acquisition of knowledge is easier than assessing the other two—skills and attitudes. Schools, in particular, do an excellent job of this, but far too much emphasis is placed on knowledge acquisition and regurgitation.

That is not to say that knowledge isn't important, but good teachers realize they can best help their students by focussing on the attitudes and skills.

As you can see from the relatively short amount of time spent on the Knowledge component of A.S.K. that this component is already done really well in our school systems.

## SUMMARY

Put your students to work **doing** something that forces them to address all three of the components of the A.S.K. Philosophy. Teachers should plan their units of study around all three components and assess all three when the unit is completed. A conscious effort here will produce incredible curriculum documents.

If necessary, provide the students with the knowledge and ask them to use their skills to discover their attitudes. Start with their attitudes and engage them with skilful discussion to ascertain what other people think and how their attitudes might change given new knowledge or skills. Teach a skill and actively apply it to knowledge acquisition or understanding of someone else's beliefs. The primary message here is that teachers must consciously be aware of the Attitudes, Skills, and Knowledge they teach.

The ASK Philosophy is an attempt to ensure a balanced approach to planning and teaching learners. By considering all three aspects of the theory in every lesson or unit of study, the teacher will have a balanced program for the cognitive and affective domains of learning.

The ASK Philosophy is offered as food for thought and for your reflective consideration.

## A VISION

By definition, a vision is:

Something seen otherwise than by ordinary sight…a dream or trance!

A vivid picture created by the imagination…

The act or power of imagination…

Unusual wisdom in foreseeing what is going to happen…

The act or power of seeing…

A personal vision is one's overall conception of what the educator wants the organization to stand for; what its primary mission is; what its basic, core values are; a sense of how all the parts fit together; and, above all, how the vision maker fits into the grand plan.

A dream is a form of vision. The **night dreams** are often a journey back into the **repressed unconscious. Daydreams,** on the other hand, are the occasion of a journey forward, toward **what might be, what can be, what we want to be.** Call them personal visions.

## VISIONS ARE ORGANIC, PORTABLE, AND GENERIC

**ORGANIC**  They grow from seeds to seedlings to plants. They are always changing, expanding, maturing—like you!

They often start small and grow within you.

**PORTABLE**  They can be carried with you from class to class; grade to grade; school to school; and position to position.

They may not always stay exactly the same in each position, but they are fundamentally the same.

**GENERIC**  They are often widely held beliefs…but they're yours!

They are not too specific—leave specifics for the time you wish to implement your vision.

They, of necessity, need to include other people; in particular, "significant others" who will help you.

They are your personal way of seeing the world, but at the same time based on universal truths.

## Reflection

In order to create a kind of vision of an ideal classroom, or an ideal school, or an ideal educational system, you must first take the time to REFLECT.

*The vision you create based on this reflection provides the framework within which every decision you make regarding the classroom, school, system… moves you one step close to your IDEAL!*

**"Thinking is the hardest work there is, which is the probable reason why so few people engage in it".**
*—Henry Ford*

### The Visionary Process

| | | |
|---|---|---|
| **REFLECTION** | *Head* | |
| *PAST* | | |
| **WRITING** | *Hand* | |
| *PRESENT* | | |
| **VISION** | *Heart* | |
| *FUTURE* | | |

# THREE TYPES OF REFLECTION

| | | |
|---|---|---|
| **REFLECTION ON ACTION** | = is a reflection on **past** practices, actions and thoughts | 1. How do I feel about the situation?<br>2. What went well?<br>3. What did not go as well as I expected?<br>4. What options did I consider as I selected my behaviour-actions?<br>5. What option did I choose?<br>6. How did I know what I chose to do was the best at the time and on what did I base that decision?<br>7. How did I know that another behaviour-action would not be appropriate?<br>8. What made this situation unusual?<br>9. What might I have done differently? 5. |
| **REFLECTION IN ACTION** | = is a reflection in the **present** on practices, actions and thoughts while in the midst of | 1. What cues from the person or group do I see that tell me how they are responding to my behaviour-actions?<br>2. What assumptions or inferences am I making?<br>3. What options are available? What are the possible consequences of each? What would work best in this situation?<br>4. What principles-theories are guiding me?<br>5. What is unique about this situation?<br>6. What level of direction-specificity-structure is best here? 5. |
| **REFLECTION FOR ACTION** | = is a reflection for the **future** combining the reflecting ON and the reflecting IN actions indicating what **will** happen. | 1. What did I learn that I can apply in other situations?<br>2. How did I alter my knowledge, theories, or attitudes as a result of this experience?<br>3. What did I learn from this situation that confirms my intuition?<br>4. What will I remember from the situation?<br>5. If I were in a similar situation again, how would I behave? 5. |

*"Reflective practice engages the teacher (principal-educator) in a cycle of thought and action based on professional experience portraying the teacher more as a creative artist-designer than as engineer-technician."*

*—Bud Wellington*

### Reflection as a Professional Development Activity

The following notes are based on article by Joellen Killion, Guy Todnem, Bud Wellington, and Cindy Harrison, as referred to in the bibliography.

**REFLECTION   What's the big deal? Doesn't everyone do it?**

Consider these thoughts on reflection—

**Reflection is** a rich source of continued **personal and professional growth.**

Busy people typically do not engage in formal reflection. They rarely **treat themselves** to reflective experiences **unless** they are **given some time**, some **structure**, and the **expectations to do so.**

Reflection requires two things: **conscious metacognitive processing**…and **time** to reflect.

As professionals…**reflection is a gift** we give ourselves… with rigor…with purpose…and in some formal way, so as **to reveal the wisdom embedded in our experience.**

Establishing **routines** to make time **for reflection, using** trusted **colleagues** as sounding boards, and keeping **journals** are all helpful. **Reflection is more productive when guided by a process.**

Reflective practice engages the teacher in a **cycle of thought and action** based on professional experience.

Through reflection, we **develop context-specific theories** that **further our own understanding** of our work and **generate knowledge to inform future practice.**

## Why Are Visions so Important?

1. They are the prescriptions for school reform that have the best chance to be taken seriously, enacted, and sustained by teachers and principals.

2. The visions of school people stem from rich insights through personal experience, often after many years in these self-same schools that you are trying to change.

3. Teachers should not be put in a position of implementing the ideas of "others" outside the school and with which they may not agree.

4. Teachers and principals who convey their craft knowledge and their visions to other adults derive enormous personal satisfaction and recognition. Vision unlocked is energy unlocked. Staff must be professionally recognized. Working toward personal visions for the classroom, school, system…is rewarding.

5. Many researchers are finding a consistent relationship between the presence of teachers' and principals' visions and the effectiveness of their schools. Visions should be noble, realistic, and clear!

6. By not having classroom/school visions, it invites random prescriptions for change from the outside.

## VISIONS PROVIDE  A. INCREASED ENERGY

## B. GOOD IDEAS

## C. HOPE

Increased energy, good ideas, and hope will "fix" education.

### *People are VERY INTERESTED in other people's visions.*

# WRITING AS A PROFESSIONAL DEVELOPMENT ACTIVITY

*Writing about **PRACTICE** is one of the best ways to encourage **REFLECTION** both for **STUDENTS** and **STAFF**.*

*Writing is **YOU** working one-on-one with **YOU**!*

*In order to know what I think,
I need to write what I say.*

*Writing is the doing part of thinking*

"Probably no professional development activity has as much potential for promoting reflection, clarification, articulation, discussion—and risk— as <u>writing</u>. Successful writing about practice can be an endeavor from which "everyone wins" and learns: the writer, the reader, and the school."

—Roland S. Barth, "Improving Schools From Within"

# A PERSONAL VISION OF A GOOD SCHOOL

*Paul Jackson, Elementary School Principal*

## Background

A personal vision for a school is an individual's overall conception of what that educator sees as the grand plan for the school. Visions affect every decision made every day, either consciously or unconsciously. Visions originate from past experiences combined with present knowledge and a little "crystal balling" to foresee the future.

One of the most difficult steps in "visioning" is having the courage and taking the time to record the vision. Sharing the vision is risk-taking of the highest order, but one that's needed in order to provide the incentive to lead others toward that vision.

Roland Barth, a renowned educator at Harvard University, likens visions to dreams. Not the night dreams that often take us on a journey back into the past, but daydreams that carry us "on a journey forward, toward what might be, what can be, and what we want it to be".

Any visionary statement is a growing, changing entity. A vision is in a constant state of flux. Visions don't change drastically overnight, but neither can they remain static. Visions do not include working details of future action. They are not all-inclusive.

Visions guide an individual or organization in making wiser choices. Making good choices is of paramount importance in everyone's life. With a vision in mind, it provides a framework within which all decisions have meaning while working toward long-range goals.

My personal vision of a good school is one where both students and staff want to come to work each day. This requires an upbeat positive climate where staff model positive relationships with each other; where risk-taking is considered not only safe to do, but pleasurable and rewarding; where every day you are expected to work hard and improve yourself; where laughter is prized and small successes are celebrated; where coming to school will be a pick-me-up even on a "down" day; where visitors to the school sense a warm feeling when they are in the building; where the physical environment is appealing; where ownership of the school is a shared responsibility among students, staff, parents, and the community; where students and staff are respected and respectful, and where positive self-images are enhanced.

A good school includes staff who model all the things they want the students to learn. These include but are not exclusive to:

- Working cooperatively
- Valuing, in practice, reading, writing and speaking
- Obeying and enforcing the rules and policies of the school
- Sharing the responsibility of discipline, especially self-discipline
- Treating everyone with respect
- Celebrating successes openly and with dignity
- Sharing "mistakes" and accepting the lessons learned from them

- Articulating where they are going and why (goals and means)
- Taking a leadership role
- Respecting the right of others to make choices without fear of ridicule
- Pushing yourself to be the best you can possibly be
- Being active rather than passive learners
- Behaving appropriately for the circumstances
- Caring for fellow staff and students
- Sharing knowledge
- Being "human"
- Accepting praise graciously
- Promoting the school with pride

Leadership is the sharing of knowledge, skills, and talents for the betterment of everyone. A good school is characterized by a strong leadership component—not just administrative leadership, but leadership from teachers, support staff, pupils, and parents.

### "None of us is as good as all of us!"
*—Ray Kroc*

Good schools don't blame someone else if things aren't as good as they would like them to be. School improvement comes from <u>within</u> the school community. The people who truly make a good school are those directly and actively involved. Empowered individuals who have a vested interest in a school create situations for continuous improvement. Like so many other aspects of a good school, improvement is infectious.

### As we learn we grow. As we grow we learn.

Good schools address the students' growth academically, socially, and physically. Progress in academic learning should be in evidence. Such growth should be measured relative to the individual's starting point for growth. The social component of education should reflect the realities of life. Individuals must see themselves as part of the larger picture—capable of contributing to that which is outside their personal domain, and at the same time willing to draw from this outside environment that which will make a better life for themselves. Promotion of a healthy life style attitude includes being physically active, as well as choosing activities that promote the mental well-being of individuals.

The skill of making wise choices is an important life skill. The responsibility for the consequences of those choices rests with the individual. The number one job of all persons responsible for teaching young people is to teach them how to make choices.

### Living is a series of choices—make wise ones.

Parental involvement in the teaching-learning process of formal education should be active, not passive. The responsibility for a child's education begins with the parents and that responsibility never ceases. Too much teaching is left to the "formal" process of schools, from nursery schools to universities. Parents have much to share with teachers about their child. Teachers have much to share with parents about teaching and learning. Just as learning is a life-long process, so too is the parental involvement with the child's education. The level of involvement will vary, but the most important contribution parents can make is time—time to talk to a child about what is going on in school; time to visit the school formally and informally; time to insist that the child become self-disciplined with regular learning pursuits (reading, writing, discussing, doing homework, participating in music lessons, sports and fitness); time to model the behaviors that foster learning. Parents and teachers are a team in this process and students must see it that way.

Good schools have dedicated professionals working there—staff who take learning, teaching, and leading seriously. Concepts like collaboration, professionalism, dedication, a positive outlook on life, reflective self-evaluation, risk-taking, balancing personal and professional lives, using goals to foster growth, visioning, a child-centered philosophy, life-long learning, using empathy not sympathy to deal with children, believing all children can learn, accepting change…are not just words or phrases. They are a part of the teacher's way of life—a vocation, not a job!

A good school has a staff who look beyond the classroom or school or system for innovations, ideas, and philosophies that could be used to improve education. The school does not sit isolated from the rest of the world. Educators and parents must have a global picture of the world into which the school fits. A school is not immune from the problems outside its walls. By the same token, it cannot be the cure-all for those problems. It cannot be all things to all people, yet that is the unwritten mandate. Good schools strive to accomplish that which they know cannot be accomplished.

**The Assignment**

Now that I have shared with you my vision of a good school, which was indeed organic, portable, and generic through several schools during my fifteen years as an elementary school principal, it is your turn to produce your vision.

Whether yours is a vision of a classroom, school, department, system, or any other division in the educational field, it is imperative you write your own.

There will plenty of help for you.

In the following section of this report, you will find VISION STARTERS. These starters I have named RaW Stems™. RaW Stems are open-ended statements that force reflection before writing the responses. Because they are open-ended, there is great latitude in providing responses.

There is no need to use all of these statements. They are provided to give you a starting point as you record your reflective thoughts.

Remember that whatever your vision is today, it will change tomorrow. It is still imperative that you record your vision so you may read it over and over again as you allow it to guide your every decision.

It is also important that at some time you share your vision with others. At this stage, you are taking risk-taking up a notch. By publicly sharing your vision, you put additional pressures on you to live up to that vision.

I know from personal experience that sharing my vision of a good school with my staff had many more pluses than minuses while making decisions on a day-to-day basis. It also helped clarify decision-making regarding the direction the school was moving, the responses to teacher requests, the disciplining of the students, the way in which I dealt with parents, the atmosphere in the school, and the importance of professional development.

I trust each of you will get to the point of sharing your vision with others!

**Begin immediately to write your personal/professional vision of a good school, classroom, division, system...by listing those characteristics that you think are absolutely essential.**

Read the "vision starters" below to get you started with the writing process. Take your time. Make changes. Ponder and reflect. JUST DO IT!

# VISION STARTERS

## What is your vision for your school, classroom, system...?

What is your response?

How do you react?

What do you say?

I believe we all have a vision for our school or classroom, but we are not always able to articulate it, especially on short notice. We may not have taken the time to tie together those ideas and ideals that would make up our vision. We may not have taken the time to truly reflect on our beliefs and experiences, and certainly most of us have never taken the time to actually articulate our vision in writing or share it with someone else. Why not?

*Thinking stems for administrators to assist in writing:*

"When I leave this school, I would like to be remembered for..."

"I want my school to become a place where..."

"The kind of school I would like my own children to attend would..."

"The kind of school where I would like to teach would..."

"If I could change something about my school it would be..."

"The reason I chose an administrative position in the teaching profession was to make a difference. I could make that difference by..."

"I look at my students (or staff) and I wish that…"

"I've always thought that _________ should be occurring in schools."

"We're doing a good job at _________ but we could do a better one by…"

"What would happen within the school if…"

"With a little leadership on my part I believe we could…"

"In reflecting on last year I'd like to…"

"If an educational magazine were to describe my ideal school they would say…"

## There is doing and not doing. There is no such thing as trying.

*Thinking stems for teachers to assist the writing:*

"In an ideal classroom, the teacher and students would…"

"My role in the classroom is…"

"The role of my classroom in the school context is…"

"Risk-taking is important to me, so…"

"Process versus product in my classroom leans more toward _________________________________________ "

"Teaching is…"

"Past experiences with students of this age tell me that…"

"Society in general is reflected in my classroom as…"

"Parents would like to see…"

"Through the curriculum my students will learn…"

"If I could change something about my classroom…"

"What would happen in my classroom if…"

"I'm doing a good job at…but it could be better if…"

"The reason I chose teaching was to make a difference. I could make that difference by…"

"In reflecting on last year I'd like to…"

"If nothing else, when my students leave my classroom they will realize (know, appreciate, be expected to)…"

"My personal/professional reputation as a classroom teacher should include the fact that I…"

"Among my many roles as a "classroom teacher", the most important are…"

"In teaching students 'about life' so they may grow to be as good as they can be, I will focus on…"

"Students coming in to my classroom for the first time should already know from former students and their parents that…"

# APPENDIX

## A THOUSAND MILES

*An excerpt from "Improving Schools from Within" by Roland S. Barth, pp. 158–9*

I travelled a thousand miles to find a vision. I came to the citadel of learning, for surely Harvard would have the vision I needed. I asked and probed and thought and reflected. I questioned and looked from person to person.

I found visions. Many of them. They came in all sorts of shapes and sizes. They were large ones and modest ones. There were complex ones and simple ones. They all seem to fit—yet none of them fit me. Why?

Then I remembered that I once had a vision—a vision that was my very own. Where had it gone? What had I done with it? So I started searching those long dark corridors of past years.

I found my vision. Rusty, dirty from lack of care—but still there. It was my vision, a vision not exactly like everyone else's. With the power to carry me forward, to shine light on the path of the future—for me and for those with whom I might share my vision.

And I learned an important lesson. I learned that each of us must have a vision. It must be uniquely ours. For until we have a vision to share, we can't understand anyone else's. I learned I must keep my vision polished brightly through daily attention, or I will lose it again. That it can act as a guiding beacon only as long as I hold it in front of me.

And I discovered that I can look to myself. That I am rich in resources and thoughts and ideas. That the future, my future, lies not out there, but inside me.

# CLASSROOM MANAGEMENT

*Marjan Glavac*

## What do I do the first day of school?

### Presumptions:

### Best Time to Prepare for the First Day /First Week/ First Term/ First Semester of School

1. Make notes during and after that first day of school.

2. Place all notes, observations, lessons, handouts, and visual aids into a First Day of School file.

3. During the school year, add anything that has to do with the first day to the file.

4. Before the new school year begins, (one to four weeks before the first day), take out your file. Review the material, update, and implement.

5. Begin the whole process again by fine-tuning what went well and what didn't.

The wonderful advantage that teaching has over other professions is that we get a fresh start every year. That first day of school comes with a new opportunity to work with a new set of students. Every year of teaching can only get better with more experience, through reflection on what worked and what didn't the year before.

Having a successful first day happens weeks, and sometimes months, before students enter your classroom. The time and effort you take to getting prepared and organized for that first day will ensure not only a smooth running first day, but a smooth running school year. The other wonderful advantage of teaching is the natural breaks during the school year. You can introduce changes and fine-tune your classroom management plans at the end of a term, such as after the Christmas/Winter Break, after the March/Spring Break, or even after a three or four day long weekend.

Every school, every teaching assignment, every classroom is unique and different. If I'm new to a school, one of the first things I like to do is to find out the unique set of opening day procedures set down by the school's administration. I want to know:

- Do students already know who their teacher is and class they're in?

- Where do I meet my students on that first day?

- Do they line up outside my room?

- Do I meet them in the gymnasium or auditorium?

- Do I meet them outside?

Usually the office administration will have a memo of guidelines for the first day. Sometimes, teachers have been doing it so long, it's automatic to them. If you're the new kid on the block, you want to find out what's expected of you. Just ask your administrator or a veteran teacher on staff.

Next, I like to have a procedure in place on what students should do with their backpacks, coats, jackets, and lunches. I want to know:

- Are there lockers, coat hooks, or room in the classroom for their belongings?

- Are lockers and coat hooks assigned or randomly chosen by students?

- If assigned, how do students get their locker or coat hook?

- If unassigned, is it first come, first served?

That first day is a very anxious day, not only for students, but for teachers as well! A procedure in place that is communicated to students will ease any anxiety and ensure a smooth flow. You want to avoid any confusion in students not knowing where to go or what to do. The last thing you want is a scramble by students for lockers or coat hooks, resulting in pushing, shoving, or even fights! Imagine the tone that would be set for your class and for you if that happened before students even set foot inside your classroom!

I found this out the hard way. One September, I was assigned a new school undergoing an increase in student population. There were never enough coat hooks for every student in the school. That first day was horrendous! Students wanted to hang up their coats and backpacks. Since there weren't enough coat hooks, backpacks ended up in the hallway or were brought into the class and blocked student movement. Students stepped on and tripped over the backpacks. Tempers flared. Words were exchanged—"He stepped on my backpack on purpose!" "No, I didn't!" "Yes, you did!" You get the idea.

Eventually some extra coat hooks were found for students down the hallway with another class. Although that solved one problem, it brought up a whole set of new problems. There were a number of students who became separated from their class, and since the hallway was designed in a circle, the students were now around the curve of the circle and far enough away that they couldn't be directly supervised by their own classroom teacher. The teacher who now "inherited" these new students wasn't too happy about getting more students to supervise along with her own. Eventually, a whole set of new coat racks was built to accommodate students.

I give this example to show how one little detail can throw you off and disorientate students. It also shows students that if you can't be organized for them before they even get to class, what hope is there for the rest of the year?!

It's the same for the inside of the classroom:

- Are there enough desks and other furniture?

- If you need more desks or furniture, where do you go to get them?

- If you have too much furniture, what do you do with it?

- Do you have enough textbooks, notebooks, and other classroom supplies?

- If you don't have enough supplies, how do you get more?

- If you ordered the classroom supplies, did they arrive?

In my second year of teaching, I was in a new school. There weren't enough grammar textbooks for every student. I failed to mention this to my principal. So, I had students share them. A number of parents complained to the principal that the shortage of textbooks was unacceptable to them and to their children. The principal ended up ordering the extra textbooks, but not before I made him look bad in front of the parents. It was one more obstacle I didn't need as a new teacher to overcome with some of my parents.

Other considerations for the class include:

- How you want the layout of the room to look like?

- Do you want desks in rows, in groups, or in a horseshoe arrangement?

- Do you want to start in rows, then move into another arrangement?

- Where do you want the teacher's desk?

- Do you want the teacher's desk facing students or in the back of the room?

- Do you want to be beside the doorway?

- Where do you want your files and teacher materials?

- Where do you want students to hand in materials?

- How are consumable materials accessed—by the teacher, by your students?

- Where are consumable materials? Out in the open or behind a locked cabinet?

When setting up your classroom, think of where the high traffic areas are located. Try to anticipate any bottlenecks when students are entering and leaving the classroom.

A good idea is to have most frequented files and materials close to you or in a separate file drawer for ease of access.

- How do you want your reading, writing, and/or computer centers set up?

- How do you want work areas for student groups set up?

- Where do you want to store ongoing student projects?

Make sure there is enough area around your centers for students to easily move about.

Here is a sample of how my classroom is set up, and my procedures and routines for the first day.

## Being Proactive

I prefer to set the standard myself and avoid as many problem situations as I can by being as proactive as possible that first day.

Even before class begins on that first day, I have already set up the desks in rows. I have already neatly printed the names of students on construction paper and taped to the front of their desks. I also have set up four extra seats with materials and assignments for students who register late and haven't made it onto my list. Based on what I already know about my students, I've placed them according to where they can learn the best. Students who need extra attention from me are placed close to my desk. Already a number of assignments are waiting for them on their desk. There is an agenda and instructions on the board. I have sharpened two pencils and placed them, along with an eraser, on their desks.

I meet my students outside with a sign indicating my grade. I'm also wearing a name tag for students and parents who may not know who I am. I'm out there early, mingling and greeting former students, students I already know, and the parents. Since there are usually a lot of parents that first day, it's a good idea to briefly introduce yourself and make a great impression.

I call out the names of the students from my class list and ask them to line up one behind another. When the last student is in line, I tell them where we'll be going. I also ask them how they should behave when we are going to class. My expectation is that we are all quiet and walking to the classroom.

This is an opportune time to reinforce your expectations and your standards before you even reach the classroom. If the group is too noisy, go back outside and repeat the procedure.

Once we get to the classroom, each student is assigned a coat hook for their backpacks. I also tell them to take out their lunches if they brought them and place them in the lunch bin.

I greet each student at the door by asking his or her name, checking its correct pronunciation, and confirming they are on the class list. This reassures the student that they're in the right class with the right teacher.

Then, I shake every student's hand and tell them to quickly and quietly take their seats and begin working on the assignment on their desk. I wait to see if each student complies. If the student is not quiet, I wait until he/she is settled at his/her desk before I go on to the next student. If a student does not comply and is talkative, I call the student back and repeat my expectations in a calm, normal voice. In this way, by the time all the students have entered the class and been seated, all have complied to a number of my instructions even before I've introduced the rules of the class. I have also set the standard as to how and what they are to do when they enter the class. This is the same procedure I follow every day. However, after the first day, instead of shaking their hand, I usually ask them a review question from either a previously taught lesson or an upcoming lesson, and check their planners or homework.

Once this routine is in place, students will be eager to answer a question. They will also remind you if you don't ask them a question! It's a great way to do some one-on-one instruction with a student, check their moods, and find out more about each student in an informal and non-threatening manner.

## Planting the Seeds

The first day is also a great opportunity to "plant a seed" with your high-needs students. Since I've already identified a number of students who have had behavior and academic difficulties in the past, I usually extend my hand, look them in the eye, say their name, and tell them that they will have a great year. Your complimentary and positive attitude may be the first one the student has heard in a long, long time! You may be the only positive figure in this student's life.

Once students are all quietly working and completing their first assignment, I ask them to put their pencils down and have their "eyes on me". I then introduce myself, my expectations, and the rules of the class.

Some teachers prefer to have the students set up rules, through consensus or through voting. Other teachers prefer to set up the rules themselves and then discuss and teach them to the students. There are merits in each approach. Again, which you choose depends on how comfortable you feel. From the outset, I want to send students the message that I am setting the standard because I am ultimately responsible for teaching them. Later in the year, as I get to know them and as they get to know me, the rows of desks will change to groups and students will have more responsibility in managing the classroom.

## Class Rules

How many rules should there be? It's a good idea to have as few as possible. I try to limit the posted rules to six. The more rules you have, the more you need to enforce them. Take this opportunity to discuss what routines and procedures are, and why they are so important. We talk about their daily morning routine and why it's important to have a routine. Then we talk about the daily routines in class and why they are important.

These six rules are the basis of my discipline code. I also explain what discipline means. Students think it's punishment. I tell them that it's doing what's right when no one is watching. When introducing the rules, I make sure my tone and body language is serious and business like. I try very hard not to make a joke or laugh when introducing these rules. If you want students to be serious about your rules, your actions should be congruent with your words. Lead by example.

Here are my Rules of the Class:

1. Be in assigned seat and ready to work.

2. Bring all equipment and assignments.

3. Keep hands, feet, books, and objects to yourself.

4. Use appropriate language.

5. Follow teacher's instructions.

6. No food or gum in the classroom.

Each rule also has a consequence:

- FIRST TIME: Name on board. Warning.

- SECOND TIME: One check beside name. Fifteen minute detention.

- THIRD TIME: Two checks beside name. Thirty minute detention.

- FOURTH TIME: Three checks. Forty-five minute detention. Phone call to parents.

Instead of a phone call to parents, you may want to have the student write, print, or dictate the information to the parent. In this way, the student also practices letter writing.

This also gives me the chance to tell them what a detention really means. It comes from the French word *detendre*—a lessening of tension. It's a chance to cool down and consider how to make good decisions. When we're upset, emotions rule us instead of logic, making us say things that we later regret!

I also give rewards for good behavior. These include positive notes and comments to students and parents, free time, extended recesses, no homework, extra reading time, extra Physical Education, game time, class parties, sending students to the office for a sticker, and a pat on the back.

As I mentioned, I don't smile when explaining the rules. I do smile and laugh and joke when I explain the rewards.

## *Examples of first day handouts*

# Building Rapport

Name _______________________

Date _______________________

### Making New Friends

Find a classmate who fits each of these descriptions. Ask that person to sign on the line.

Even if you don't fill all the boxes, see how many different names you can get and how many new friends you can meet.

| | |
|---|---|
| 1. Is taller than you | 20. Has freckles |
| 2. Is left-handed | 21. Has a birthday this month |
| 3. Walks to school | 22. Has traveled to two states |
| 4. Has curly hair | 23. Has long hair |
| 5. Has no sisters or brothers | 24. Was born in another country |
| 6. Has initials that spell a word | 25. Lives in an apartment |
| 7. Was born in your city | 26. Wears glasses |
| 8. Is new to your school | 27. Takes music lessons |
| 9. Went camping this summer | 28. Can whistle |
| 10. Is the oldest in the family | 29. Just moved to a new home |
| 11. Has an unusual pet | 30. Has seen two oceans |
| 12. Collects stamps | 31. Is the youngest in the family |
| 13. Has blue eyes | 32. Has a smart phone |
| 14. Was in your class last year | 33. Has been a hospital patient |

| | |
|---|---|
| 15. Is on a sports team | 34. Loves to read |
| 16. Has been to Disney World | 35. Has red hair |
| 17. Has an eight letter name | 36. Has a tooth missing |
| 18. Collects coins | 37. Has eaten a strange food |
| 19. Has had a broken arm | 38. Hasn't talked with you before |

And finally ___________________ is really an expert about

___________________________________________ .

*Examples of First Day handouts*

## Discipline: Rules and Procedures

1. Visualize the kind of class you would like to have. Think about what students need to do to make this happen. List the rules and procedures to help make this happen.

_______________________________________________

_______________________________________________

_______________________________________________

_______________________________________________

_______________________________________________

_______________________________________________

_______________________________________________

2. How do you want to arrange your class desks? In single, double, or triple rows? Will they be in groups? Will they be in a horseshoe formation?

_______________________________________________

_______________________________________________

_______________________________________________

3. What are your procedures for:

    a) Entering the classroom, and opening and closing the door?

    b) Exiting the classroom for dismissal? For an emergency drill?

    c) Arriving early or late for class?

d) When another adult enters the classroom?

e) When you are speaking to another adult inside or outside of the classroom?

f) When students are finished their work early?

g) How to ask a question?

h) Going to the washroom?

i) Getting a drink of water?

j) Listening to announcements?

k) Getting ready for the next lesson?

l) When there is a substitute teacher?

m) Sharpening your pencil?

n) Getting materials such as paper, scissors, glue, etc.

o) When someone is feeling ill, or upset?

p) When someone needs a bandage?

q) Getting into partners/groups?

r) Going to the library?

s) Movement in the hallways?

t) Going to another classroom for a different subject?

u) Preparing for special classes such as physical education, music, and science and technology?

v) Taking play equipment for recess?

w) Taking attendance?

x) Catching up on missed work?

y) Leaving class early for an appointment?

z) Use of the telephone?

4. Other procedures unique to your school and classroom.

# The Class Snapshot

*Paul Jackson*

## The Concept of a Class Snapshot

As classroom teachers, we get to know our students as the year progresses. The information comes from a variety of sources, including school records, previous teachers, report cards, personal experience with the student, outside agencies that deal with the students, parents...

It is imperative that you have at your fingertips as much information about each individual student as possible. One of the problems is, how do you gather and record that information without it becoming a burden and without the relevant data overwhelming you?

In dealing with classroom teachers, as a school administrator, it was sometimes obvious to me that the classroom teachers were being overwhelmed with the needs of the students because they had not stopped to really analyze where the problems were and how many students were responsible for the problems in the classroom. When you have data readily available, you can quickly come to the realization, for example, that there were not nearly as many serious behavior problems as the teacher thought once she actually looked at the students individually.

By focusing on the students who did require intervention and realizing that the majority of the students were actually well behaved gives the teacher hope that by working on the two or three students who did require intervention, she could remarkably reduce the classroom disruptions and thus create a better learning environment for everyone. In other words, it wasn't the whole class that was misbehaving, but rather only two or three key students. This is powerful information in making decisions about what to do and with whom to work.

**CAUTION**: It may not be advantageous to share this kind of information in its completed form with anyone or everyone. You are the best judge of that. There is nothing wrong with collecting this data as outlined below. Remember, the data is designed to give you a better Snapshot of your class in order to make better decisions when it comes to how you manage your classroom. The Snapshot is a "tool" for your personal/ professional use.

## A Suggested Format for the Class Snapshot Data Collection

The suggestions outlined below will be very useful to you as a classroom teacher. The basic idea is that you prepare "cheat-sheets" of information in a very condensed fashion for each of your students. Using codes for the various criteria that you are assessing for each student, you create a summary sheet of information.

At this point, it might be a good idea to take a quick look at the forms included in this report. They are located at the end of this introduction. Skim them to get an idea of what they are all about, then come back here to find out more about the kind of information you could/should collect and how you can use this information to its greatest advantage for you and your students.

By having this kind of data at your fingertips at all times, you are empowering yourself with each and every decision you make regarding your students and the classroom in general. You should feel an increased confidence when discussing individuals and the class in general.

All of the data collected for individual students can be quantified if necessary to give a Snapshot of your class. For example, you could tally the special needs students who are withdrawn from your class on a regular basis and use this information to give a percentage number or a ratio of special needs withdrawal students compared to the entire class.

You can also tally several criteria categories to create an overall picture of inter-related issues or criteria. For example, you may wish to tally all students in your class who require individual instruction in some form or other during a typical day which could include English as a Second Language, learning disorders, ADD or ADHD, or any other criteria you may wish to include.

**What data should you collect?**

The data you choose to record is entirely up to you. Create your own codes and add to the list provided. **Record only what is relevant to the student for your use as a classroom teacher.** For some students, the data collected will be minimal; for others, very extensive information will be necessary.

The data will change over the course of the school year. It is suggested that you begin the school year by gathering as much information as possible, as soon as possible. Having as much data as possible for the first day of school will make your start to the school year a smoother one. You may also eliminate changes you might normally make during the first few weeks of school.

Your primary source of information will be the students' school records passed on to you by the previous teacher. There are many other sources of information as listed above.

Here are some suggested criteria to look for with each and every student:

English as a Second Language (ESL)

Language Difficulties

Speech Problems

Enrichment Program

Remedial Programs

Supervision Requirements

Group Work

Reliability

Family History

Educational History

Special Needs Programs

Medical History

Behavior Problems

Outside Agencies

Subject Marks—Academic Strength

You can add others that are relevant to you, your students, and your school.

# The Benefits of the Class Snapshot

**How can having this kind of data be of benefit to you?**

1. In creating a seating plan, you can use this data to establish a plan that is most conducive to your teaching style and the needs of the students.

2. Conferences with parents, school administrators, other teachers, students, special needs teachers, and outside agencies are much easier to prepare for and much easier to conduct when you have so much data readily available. You can add information if necessary for specific conferences but that is easier than starting from scratch. And if you keep your Snapshot up to date, you can report on progress or a lack of progress with authority.

3. The class Snapshot data is portable. It is not necessary to carry pages and pages of information with you. Your information is on only a few sheets of paper and/or stored on your computer. You have the data readily available no matter where you are working.

4. Some parts of the data collected on the Class Snapshot Sheets can be very useful in preparing for supply (substitute) teachers. You can choose which data is imperative for supply teachers to know. One suggestion is that you prepare a Supply Teacher Kit that you keep updated so if you require a day away from school, the preparation for your absence is minimal. Leave this Kit at school.

5. Report card writing will be made easier using the data sheets and the student notes you have compiled. The criteria are most assuredly areas that both the student and

the parents will want to hear something about. It should be much easier to write the reports and easier to get started when you have so much information at your fingertips.

6.  The Snapshot allows teachers to track progress as the year progresses. You can physically stroke out items that are no longer applicable. You can modify your notes to indicate specific evidence of progress. You can use dated information to your advantage to corroborate interventions you have initiated and with whom you have initiated them.

7.  Having the Snapshot sheets available to you will make conferring with last year's teachers of your students to gather pertinent information a focused and streamlined process. And next year's teachers of your students will benefit from your Snapshot in helping them deal with the students they are receiving.

**CAUTION**: I would advise you against simply photocopying your Snapshot sheets and giving them to another teacher. That would leave the information open to too much interpretation. You and only you understand why you recorded what you did and why you chose certain interventions. You must protect the integrity of **your** data collection. It is the ethical moral and professional approach.

8.  The Snapshot data could very effectively be used to set goals for your classroom related to curriculum and/or classroom behavior. The information provided helps you focus on the "needs" of the students individually and collectively. It is important to have classroom goals and to share them with the students. It is equally important to share with the class why you are setting those goals, bearing in mind you must do this tactfully and with age-appropriateness.

9.  If you are called upon to justify to yourself or others the rationale of doing what you are doing in the classroom, the data in the Snapshot will be invaluable. Nothing convinces others of the legitimacy of your argument than "cold hard facts". And these facts can be quantified, if necessary, to make your point. Percentages are often more impressive than actual numbers.

10. The Snapshot is a readily available quick reference for the classroom teacher without having to go searching through school records or other information. You can always provide backup corroboration if necessary, but armed with relevant data from the Snapshot that is unlikely to be needed. Don't forget that you can modify the data collecting instrument to suit yourself.

11. Teachers employing the Snapshot data collecting instrument have an increased feeling of "being on top of things"; of "being in control". So the Snapshot is a stress reducer. It is justification for your actions. It is taking action with forethought and relevant information. It is empowering. It is impressive.

12. Snapshot information reduces the likelihood that a teacher will say that she/he has a really "bad class" as opposed to having a class with "some problems" that will require some attention. The more specific you are about describing the problems of your class, and there are always problems, the more likely you are to spend the time and energy to eliminate or reduce the problems.

13. When a classroom teacher has the Snapshot data in front of him/her, it becomes more evident of the strengths of the class as well. This is an area that teachers often forget to assess. It is imperative that you stop and look at the positive side of the data collected. Your classroom can be

unique in a positive way as well. For every percentage of students who have behavioral problems (15%), there are a number of students who don't have them (85%). Do take some time to list the strengths. Build on those strengths. Use them to your advantage as a teacher and to help students in need.

14. You will likely discover that the majority of your students are okay, doing well, coping as well as can be expected, meeting their own needs, working at capacity, and feeling good about themselves. It really helps to have this positive image of your individual students and the class as a whole.

15. Snapshot data will help you assess what you need to do and whether or not you need additional help with the needs of the class. It's important for you to do the initial assessment and important that you provide your data to win the argument for additional help when you request it. Your success rate in asking for additional support will be better with this data.

16. Use the Snapshot data to help you create your groups for work in the classroom. If you employ "teams" in your classroom to handle the jobs and responsibilities of running the class, the data will be useful here. It is often a better idea to pick the teams based on what each of them brings to the group. If possible, try to include team members that will contribute in a positive way in at least one area of the individual's strengths.

17. If you employ any form of "student tutor" (coach, helper, mentor) system in the classroom where students who have special abilities can act as resource people for the other students, the Snapshot data can be helpful here as well. I recommend using some form of student tutor system.

If you do, make sure that the tutors are well trained in what they can and cannot do for the students seeking help. Establish guidelines for the students requesting help and for the student tutors who are giving it. The classroom teacher is always the first resource to seek out, but student tutors can be invaluable in a classroom. Get permission from the parents of tutors so they realize that it is a compliment to the student chosen to tutor and that the tutoring will not interfere in that student's progress.

18. It is very important that the Snapshot information be reviewed and updated at least four times per year, or more often as the situation warrants. This should not be a time-consuming task. It is recommended that you initiate your Snapshot and have it completed no later than the end of the second week of school. It is never too late to introduce this system. The second formal review of the original data should be after the first set of report cards, then after the second set of report cards and at the end of the school year. Depending on your school timetable this could be varied. It is important to do it at the end of the year as well because that should lead you to set some teacher goals for the next teaching year even though the students will be different.

19. Take the time at the end of each year to reflect using the Snapshot. Consider the successes first and foremost. Look at each student in terms of the progress made. Congratulate yourself and the others who assisted you. Send thank-you notes to those who helped make "you" a success. Congratulate your students for their progress. Take a look at the Snapshot process itself and write yourself a note about what changes to make for next year. Personalize the entire process of data collection

and analysis, which is what the Snapshot really is. Make a determined effort for "continuous improvement" in the system. Share the system with others. There is nothing more rewarding than helping someone else make their teaching experience a more positive one. Become an advocate for change, for working smarter not harder, for being in control.

## THE KEY POINTS

1. The systematic collection of relevant data makes the teaching and learning experience a better one.

2. Knowledge is power. And power is comforting.

3. Personalizing this Class Snapshot system is imperative.

4. Change is inevitable. Good change is even better.

5. The return on your investment of time in creating the Snapshot will be worth the effort.

6. Take the moral and professional high road in collecting, using, sharing, and recording of the data.

7. Once you have the data, use it to benefit you and your students.

| Class Snapshot Student Summary Sheet | | | |
| --- | --- | --- | --- |
| **#** | **Student Name**<br>**Parents' Names**<br>**Phone Number** | **Codes** | **Notes** |
| | | | |
| Ex. | Joey Somebody<br>Marilyn and Todd<br>764-9008 | g, f, SP | Good leader in group work.<br>Family new to the school.<br>Hearing aid with special classes once a week on Wed. P.M. (withdrawal). |
| | | | |
| | | | |
| | | | |

| Class Snapshot Codes | |
| --- | --- |
| **Code/Symbol** | **Description** |
| **Notes** | The following are provided as examples only. Your personal/professional circumstances will dictate what is relevant to you and your situation.<br><br>You will notice that capital letters in the codes indicate more serious problems than lower case letters so you can readily see the seriousness of the problem.<br><br>It is NOT necessary to record a code beside each student's name. Only record what is relevant to you and the student. |
| L<br><br><br><br>l | **Language problems — major** enough to require additional assistance, withdrawal, or outside agencies. This could include speech problems, speaking a foreign language at home, or being new to the country.<br><br>**Language problems of a minor nature** that can be dealt with in the classroom by modifying the assignments and expectations. |
| EN<br><br><br><br><br>en | **Enrichment student with a formal acknowledgement** from the school district—may or may not be attending special classes for enrichment. The classroom teacher may be expected to modify the program to meet the needs of this student.<br><br>**Enrichment without the formal designation** but still requiring some modification of the program in order to meet the needs of the student. |
| R<br><br><br><br><br>r | **Remedial student formally identified** as requiring a special program either through withdrawal from the class or accommodated within the classroom. The needs of the student could be anything from a learning disability to a personality disorder as long as it has been formally identified.<br><br>**Remedial student who has not been formally identified** but is known to require remediation in some form in order to function well in the classroom. This student has identifiable needs not a student who is necessarily generally weak with a low IQ, but that could also be the case. |

| Class Snapshot Codes | |
| --- | --- |
| **Code/Symbol** | **Description** |
| S | **Constant supervision is required for this student** regardless of the reasons for it. This is the student who may have a teacher's aide assigned to her/him on a full or part-time basis. This may also be a student who has a parent volunteer work with her/him on a regular basis. |
| s | **Some supervision or additional help is required** for this student which may be additional help by the teacher or a student tutor assigned to provide additional help. |
| G | **When creating groups for work in the classroom this student requires special considerations** in order to maximize the learning of the student. He/she requires good students in the group to keep this student on task without disruption to the group. They are "hard to place" students in group work. They require additional help in learning group work skills. |
| g | **These students in group work are your leaders.** They have the best skills for group work and are your group leaders. These students set the tone for the group exhibiting leadership skills that need to be taught and exemplified. |
| F | **Family history or current problems that may seriously affect the student's progress.** This may include a newborn child in the family, having recently moved, a known medical problem with a family member, financial problems, loss of a job by the parent(s), or anything else that may affect the emotional well-being of the student. Be careful how much you write in your notes. |
| f | **Family history or current problems that may affect the student's progress but not of a serious nature.** These are the kind of problems where an adjustment period may be necessary. For example, the parents may be away on vacation and the grandparents are looking after the child, or a neighbor/ relative is looking after the child on a temporary basis so routines are disrupted. |

| Class Snapshot Codes | |
| --- | --- |
| **Code/Symbol** | **Description** |
| ED | **The student's educational history warrants special attention.** The history is one that will be with the student for the entire year. The student may have repeated a grade last year or is coming off a year when much of the school year was missed due to illness or being out of the country for a long period of time. It could also be a student who was an "age promotion" where leaving her/him in the same grade wouldn't be in the best interests of the student. In other words, the history seriously affects the student. |
| ed | **The student's educational history warrants some attention.** The history recorded is likely to affect the student on a short-term basis, not long-term. The problem could be simply an adjustment to a full day instead of a half day of classes or withdrawal from a special program or reintegration into a regular classroom. This may also include a January birthday if moving into Senior Kindergarten or Grade One. |
| B | **Major behavioral problems are identified with this student that will require serious and regular intervention.** The problems will have been formally identified through a medical problem or through assessments in the educational community. The student's reputation, past behavior patterns, and formal interventions will have been a part of the student's history. These problems are serious ones requiring a team approach to manage them. Anger management may be one example. |
| b | **Minor behavioral problems are identified with student that may require intervention on an occasional basis.** The problems are disruptive but not necessarily on a regular basis. These problems may be a lack of self-control on the school yard or not working well in groups or defiant behavior on occasion. These problems may become goals for the year for the student and the teacher. |

| Class Snapshot Codes | |
| --- | --- |
| **Code/Symbol** | **Description** |
| SP | **This student is currently involved in a special program offered through the school or an outside agency during regular school hours (withdrawal) or out of school hours.** These are programs where there is a necessity to have communication between the classroom teacher and the people responsible for delivery of the program. The program may also require modification of the regular program to meet the needs of the student. |
| Sp | **This student requires a special program or intervention that may be initiated by the classroom teacher without a formal involvement of another agency or department.** This may involve working with parents or the librarian in the school or a temporary intervention by a special assignment teacher in the school on a short-term basis. The problems are short-term. |
| M | **Medical problems are of such a nature as to affect the student on a regular basis.** This may include the use of a wheelchair, oxygen tanks, a special teacher's assistant, epi-pen usage in emergencies, severe allergies (peanut butter), or anything that requires modification of the program and/or expectations for the student. It may also require special training for the teacher(s) involved with the student. |
| m | **Minor medical problems for the student require teacher awareness without it drastically affecting the expectations of the student.** This may include a hearing problem or vision problem that requires special placement in the seating plan. It may also include restricted involvement in certain activities such as running in the fall (allergies) or medications that must be taken daily at school. |

# Curriculum Planning for the School Year

*Paul Jackson*

## Presumptions

1. There is too much curriculum provided to teachers that they are expected to teach.

2. Most curriculum documents contain enough material for teachers to pick and choose what it is they can teach.

3. As a classroom teacher, you are have a legal and moral responsibility to teach all of the curriculum that the Department of Education provides to you.

4. To leave some units of study/topics out during the year short-changes your students and creates problems later in their education.

5. It is a difficult (almost impossible) job to try to teach everything expected of you.

6. In order to survive and thrive with curriculum expectations, you must take a minimalist approach to curriculum. This means that you must constantly look at the minimal amount of time spent to teach the minimal amount of content for each and every unit of study/topic you must teach. You do this not by ignoring what it is you have to do, but rather do what you have to do in a minimalist way.

7. Minimalizing the content is not compromising quality, but it is reducing the quantity of material you cover in the classroom.

8. In each unit of study/topic, you must build in to your planning schedule two very important aspects of curriculum delivery: first, make sure sufficient time is allowed for assessment with the allotted time frame if testing is a part of the unit of study; second, allow at least one period or half a period, if periods are longer in duration, for "unplanned interruptions". By planning for interruptions you will not be put off your yearly planning schedule.

9. The examples used in this document are elementary school ones but can equally apply to secondary school or college with modifications.

10. Most teachers have their "favorite" lessons or units of study that they just love to teach. Mine was the novel "Shane". Other teachers like putting on drama productions. Some teachers like their maple syrup unit with accompanying field trip. Integrate if at all possible. There is usually no place for "extra" units in most curriculum planning. BUT if the planning is done well, you can probably accommodate your special activity. By using a year-long planning schedule as outlined below, you find a way!

11. One general suggestion is to consider the language arts component of the curriculum as one that can definitely be integrated into other subject areas. With some forethought and planning you can "kill two birds with one stone" teaching the language component in other subject areas. Create assignments that can be assessed for both social studies (for example, Pilgrims) and creative writing (A Diary of a Pilgrim Father).

## The 4-Step Approach to School Year Curriculum Planning

*Step 1*        *Create Your Weekly or Bi-weekly Instructional Timetable*

1.1    Based on the time allocations for each of the subject areas, you are responsible for teaching create your weekly timetable.

**Note 1:**    Consider a two-week schedule with a Week 1 and Week 2 format that may allow you to schedule larger blocks of time for each subject. This can sometimes be more effective than a weekly schedule of smaller blocks of time.

*Step 2    Curriculum Documents—Topics and Units of Study*

2.1    Gather together all the curriculum documents you are expected to teach during the school year.

2.2    Under each subject heading, list all of the topics/units of study you must teach.

2.3    Beside each of the topics/units of study, record the number of minutes of instruction, the number of weeks, or the number of periods of instruction you are required to spend teaching the unit material.

**Note 1:**    If minutes aren't prescribed, use your best judgement as to the number of instructional periods you will need for the unit of study.

2.4    On a "yearly" calendar covering the school months, block in the number of weeks and/or periods you will require for each unit of study. See the attached example.

**Note 2:**    Color coding the units of study will be helpful.

**Note 3:**    Consider also in which season or which school term you will most likely teach that unit of study, as some units must be taught at certain times and before or after other units of study.

EXAMPLE

| Subject | Social Studies–Grade 6 |
| --- | --- |
| Topic/Unit | The Pilgrims |
| Time Allocation | 120 instructional minutes (3 periods of 40 minutes) |
| Dates for Teaching | Week 3 in September–3 Social Studies periods |

2.5    Do this with ALL subjects and all curriculum documents until you have every subject area clearly mapped out on one piece of paper. You have now assured yourself (and others) that you will cover all the curriculum expected of you.

**Note 4:**    The time spent in planning your entire year's work is time well spent. You have already reduced the time you would have spent in playing catch up at the end of the year, reduced your time gathering materials which you could share with other teachers in your division or subject area, and set your mind at ease that you can now relax about end of the year curriculum pressures.

*Step 3   Planning the Individual Units of Study*

3.1    For each topic/unit of study, determine the learning outcomes from the curriculum documents that you ABSOLUTELY MUST TEACH.

**Note 1:**    These learning outcomes may be called benchmarks, objectives, skills sets, outcomes, targets, or some other label. They are usually outlined in the introduction of the unit of study and lessons are provided that address those outcomes.

**Note 2:**    Take a "minimalist" approach to teaching for EACH OF THOSE OBJECTIVES. Teach to only those objectives that are absolutely necessary. Teach only one lesson to each of those objectives. If possible, combine many objectives in one lesson.

**Note 3:**   Use the materials provided by the curriculum documents if at all possible to save you time and effort. Minimize your preparation time. Think efficiency. Pick and choose what works best for you and your students.

**Note 4:**   Use the KISS (Keep It Simply Simple) method when preparing the lessons. Don't do more work than the students will be required to do.

**Note 5:**   Plan all of the lessons at the same time so you know you will have covered everything expected of you with a minimum of effort.

## *Step 4   Individual Lesson Plans*

4.1   Make sure you cover all of the mandated curriculum objectives/targets in the lessons you are preparing.

**Note 1:**   Consider the minimalist philosophy to include the philosophy that "a student shall be exposed to" rather than "a student shall master" whatever it is you are teaching. Teaching to mastery for each individual student is unrealistic. Take the worry out of curriculum management and coverage.

**Note 2:**   Your job as a teacher is to provide learning opportunities based on curriculum guidelines. It is not your job to ensure that every student learns everything you teach. You cannot stay on a topic/unit of study forever!

4.2   If time allows, provide "enrichment" to all the students based on the interest they have shown while teaching the unit. Expand on their interests. Take the time to include some material you, as the teacher, want to share with them. With proper planning, you can even build in a period or two to teach something special or go on a field trip or have a guest lecturer.

4.3   <u>Always</u> adhere to your prescribed yearly planning timelines. Do not extend your time for one unit of study at the expense of another. From the Department of Education's perspective, they are all equally important and leaving any of them out will harm the student in the future. Don't "rob Peter to pay Paul".

**Note 3:**     If you can teach to all of the expected objectives within the lessons you have allocated, you should consider yourself a success. There is room for flexibility in this type of planning but be aware that you must still cover all the curriculum.

## The Curriculum Planning Calendar

The curriculum planning guide attached to this document can easily be enlarged using the office photocopier, or you can create one of your own.

Make certain that you have plenty of space to record your units of study in as much detail as necessary to work with during the school year.

The following example is for your information as a model of what you can create. You can also use a standard wall calendar to do the same thing, but it is important to have the entire year "at a glance" if at all possible.

Curriculum Planning Calendar     Teacher:     Grade:     School Year:

| Months | Sept | | Oct | | Nov | | Dec | | Jan | | Feb | | March | | Apr | | May | | June | |
|---|---|---|---|---|---|---|---|---|---|---|---|---|---|---|---|---|---|---|---|---|
| #weeks/days | 3 | 16 | 4 | 20 | 4 | 21 | 3 | 14 | 4 | 20 | 4 | 20 | 3 | 18 | 4 | 19 | 4 | 21 | 3 | 17 |
| Language Arts | | | | | | | | | | | | | | | | | | | | |
| Mathematics | | | | | | | | | | | | | | | | | | | | |
| History | | | | | | | | | | | | | | | | | | | | |
| Geography | | | | | | | | | | | | | | | | | | | | |
| Social Studies | | | | | | | | | | | | | | | | | | | | |
| Science | | | | | | | | | | | | | | | | | | | | |
| Physical Education | | | | | | | | | | | | | | | | | | | | |
| Health | | | | | | | | | | | | | | | | | | | | |
| Music | | | | | | | | | | | | | | | | | | | | |
| Art | | | | | | | | | | | | | | | | | | | | |
| Guidance | | | | | | | | | | | | | | | | | | | | |
| Special Events | | | | | | | | | | | | | | | | | | | | |

# CURRICULUM MANAGEMENT

*Marjan Glavac*

## Effective Methods for Teaching Units of Study

**Presumptions:**

The most effective way to teach is by using a variety of teaching strategies that meet the learning needs of all students, address different learning styles, and employ strategies that help students make connections from prior learning/experiences to new learning.

### 1. Setting The Stage: "Hooks and Teasers"

A week, or even two or three days before you're about to teach your new unit, use a hook or teaser to arouse student interest and curiosity. This is a method that the media have perfected with cliffhangers and hooks to arouse our curiosity to tune in later. Movies are marketed with a "trailer" that show well chosen scenes and action that compel us to go to the movie theater to see the movie.

Examples of teasers I've used to introduce new topics and teaching units:

"You learn how to walk before you learn how to climb" [a mnemonic to help students learn how to graph ordered pairs in mathematics].

"Every Dead Monkey Smells Bad Dead" [a mnemonic to help students learn division steps i.e. Every-the E stands for Estimate; Dead-the D stands for Divide; Monkey-the M stands for Multiply; Smells-the S stands for Subtract; and Bad Dead-the B and D stand for Bring Down]

A mystery box is created that contains an object that is connected to the learning unit. Students get to ask one question a day until they solve it. The box is opened and the new unit is introduced.

I reinforce these teasers before students go home by writing the mnemonics on the board for inclusion in their nightly planners and repeating the teaser before they enter the class, repeating it again before recess, and repeating it before lunch. It arouses so much interest that students can't wait to learn what it means.

## 2. Pre-Planning

Do you have all your materials, props, visual aids, notes, and resources for the unit?

How do you want the classroom set up? Will students be taught in a community circle, in rows, or in groups?

How well do you know your audience, i.e. your students? Who are your strong students, your weak students? Which students will need enrichment or extra help? Who are your behavioral concerns? What are student attitudes, knowledge and skills for this new unit?

What are the objectives of the unit? What do you want your students to know by the end of the period/day? What are your goals, your BIG idea that you want students to learn from your teaching of this unit? What attitude, skills, and knowledge do you want your students to have when they leave your class at the end of the day/year? You may want to use a pre-established rubric or one of your own based on your state or province's teaching standards.

### 3. Modeling

Students take your "temperature" every moment of the day. They're reading your body language, the words that you use, your tone of voice, right down to what you're wearing and your haircut! How you present yourself will go a long way towards how students will interact with you, each other, and the unit material. If you look like something that the cat dragged in, shoulders slumped, a look of dread on your face, and telling students that this material is boring but important, students will react negatively. If on the other hand, you're excited and enthusiastic, a smile on your face, being positive, and telling students you can't wait to teach them this unit, your students will have a different reaction. They will take your cue and model your enthusiasm.

### 4. Presentation Strategies

Now that you've aroused interest and curiosity in your students with your hooks and teasers, gathered all your resources, got to know your audience, and defined your objectives, you're ready for your students!

The key is to make connections in your students with their prior knowledge. Keep the oral explanation brief—students have a limited attention span. Aim for seven to ten minutes of verbal explanations, then change the pace. There are an incredible number of ways to connect your students to the material you want to teach!

One is by brainstorming. Have students write down everything already they know either individually, in partners, in a group, or as a whole class.

Use the Round Table technique: ask every student to contribute while sitting at their desks or arrange for all students to be in a circle. Give students the option to pass if they feel pressured/uncomfortable. By giving students this option, they will feel more comfortable to respond later when they are ready. Give students an option to respond once everyone has a turn, making them aware that it's okay if they don't reply.

Use a graphic organizer. Popular ones include the KWL technique, a three-column chart with the questions, "What Do I Know?", "What Do I Want to Know?", and "What Did I Learn?"; or the KWHL technique, a four-column chart with the questions, "What Do I Know?", What Do I Want to Know?", "How Can I Find Out?", and "What Did I Learn?"; or the KWWWL technique, a five-column chart with the questions, "What Do I Know?", "What Do I Want to Know?", "Where Can I Find Out?", "What Am I Going to Do with the Information?", and "What Have I Learned from the Experience" (or "What Would I Do Differently the Next Time?")?

On chart paper, write down questions students want answered during the unit. Have this chart paper posted in classroom for easy reference during the teaching of the unit. Answer each question when students find the answers.

Formulate your questions and extension activities using Bloom's Taxonomy. Have a copy of Bloom's Taxonomy of Higher Learning thinking questions on a handy piece of paper for easy reference while you're teaching the lesson. You can also write it on chart paper and post it on the back wall of your classroom for easy reference while you're teaching.

Share the rubric of the objectives of the lesson/unit that you decided to accomplish with the students. Have students file the objectives in their journals, planners, or workbooks. Post them in the classroom.

Show students physical samples of past assignments, anchor papers, or projects (ask other teachers on staff if you don't have any past samples).

Show them examples of A, B, C, and D assignments.

Show students the concept of adding value to a project or assignment by using a concrete example. For instance, you can use the telephone. Using a picture (or if you have an old landline telephone), ask, how do we make this better? How do we add value to it, (make it smaller, portable). What else can we add to it to make it less expensive and better (make it accessible to the Internet, have it download music, games, videos, let it take pictures, make it a video camera, let it write down stuff, have it act like a credit card/debit card so you can buy a snack or drink from a vending machine, or go into a restaurant or store and pay for something with my phone number, lets you know if one of your friends is nearby in a crowded place like a mall, arena, or concert)?

In a math workshop I once attended years ago, the teacher used an ice cream sundae to show value:

- A bowl with nothing in it would be an example of an F or incomplete.

- A plain scoop of ice cream would be an example of a D.

- A scoop of ice cream with chocolate sauce would be an example of a C.

- A scoop of ice cream with chocolate sauce and sprinkles would be an example of a B.

- A scoop of ice cream with chocolate sauce and sprinkles, whipped cream, and a cherry on top would be an example of an A.

Class discussion—why? There's more effort, more value, more time added, and more ingredients. Use this analogy to apply to student's project or assignment.

## What If...?

What if your students just aren't ready to be taught? What if they've just been distracted by an interruption and they're unsettled, inattentive, or off task?

Here's a strategy that I used with a highly energetic class I had one year. The smallest distraction would make them lose focus.

Have the students put their heads down—but not as a punishment measure. I tell them that they're not in trouble. I let them relax. Sometimes I'll turn down the lights and put on soft music (of ocean waves lapping the shore, etc.). Once students are relaxed, I'll guide them through a meditation or visualization of the goals for the unit.

Sometimes a change of venue helps as well. Going outside, or going to the gymnasium, auditorium, or out in the hallway may just be the trick to having students become more attentive.

## When the Unit is Done

Take some time as soon as possible after the unit is done to write yourself notes about the unit. For example, during my math lessons, I wrote in my teacher's textbook what parts of the lesson were too hard or too easy, and which parts needed better explanation or needed more practice. After the unit was done, I sorted all the worksheets and resources into a separate file. I placed sticky notes on the worksheets that were too hard, needed to be explained better, or needed to be deleted from the unit for next year.

OR, you can use a + − 0 system of evaluating your unit lessons. For example, use the + (plus) sign to add/fine-tune or emphasize in the unit lesson; use a – (minus) sign to subtract/take away or change in the unit lesson; and use a 0 (zero) to keep or leave alone.

You can also ask students key questions about the unit or have an oral discussion about the unit; vote on the best parts/worst parts of the unit with a show of hands or do a survey.

I used a simple survey of my students using the following three questions:

1. What worked well?

2. What didn't work well?

3. What needs to be changed?

Here are some questions that you can ask yourself to evaluate the unit:

1. The lessons that worked well were…

2. The lessons that need to be modified were…

3. Modifications should be…

4. The changes necessary for this unit are…

5. The students most enjoyed…

6. The students had difficulty with…

7. The unit of study could be improved by…

8. The best part of the unit is…

# APPENDIX

## Unit outline

Unit Topic _____________________

Unit Length _______________ days

Number of Lessons ____________

Objectives and Outcomes

1. _________________________________

2. _________________________________

3. _________________________________

4. _________________________________

5. _________________________________

| Topics | Lesson Objectives | Activities | Assessment | Resources |
|---|---|---|---|---|
|  |  |  |  |  |
|  |  |  |  |  |
|  |  |  |  |  |
|  |  |  |  |  |
|  |  |  |  |  |

# Work Smarter, Not Harder
# to Differentiate/Individualize Instruction

*Paul Jackson*

One of the problems teachers face on a daily basis is how they can meet the needs of each of their students while teaching "the class". There are no easy answers. But with a plan and a process to begin with, you can accomplish your goals. There is no single answer to the problem.

For this report, the terms *differentiated instruction* and *individualized instruction* are used synonymously. Any method of meeting the needs of individual students will be in included in the possible strategies. Any strategy you choose to used will be based on the circumstances in the classroom, the ability of the student, the experience of the teacher, the resources available, and any of a myriad of other considerations.

## General Truisms about Differentiated/Individualized Instruction

You can add your own truisms to this list based on your experiences, and I would encourage you to do just that.

There are some general truisms about differentiated/ individualized instruction that classroom teachers must accept:

- Every instructional situation is individualized because every student sees, hears, and does what she/he is capable of doing, so the method of instruction should include as many of the learning styles as possible to meet as many needs as possible. This is often overlooked but important.

- The students know where they stand in the class as to overall ability and in specific subjects. Remember this when trying to meet the needs of individual students. Grouping by ability or giving additional help to specific students is perfectly understood and accepted by students. Handle it with professional aplomb and you will succeed.

- Instructional groups in your class can be "formally" established by the teacher or "informally" recognized by the student and teacher. Consider carefully the "names" of the groups to avoid negative labelling. Share with the students openly and honestly why you made the groups the way you did. Whenever possible, move students between the groupings during the year so students realize they can move "up" or "down" or "laterally" based on specific subjects and progress made or lost. Students with specific abilities should be given every opportunity to let those abilities publicly "shine".

- Individualized/differentiated instruction can be accomplished best with forethought and planning. You must consciously establish your methods of individualized instruction. Do what works! Do what works for you! Do what works for your students!

- Never individualize instruction if it means more work for the teacher than for the student. It won't be worth it. The student in these instructional situations should be expected to do the work. So creating lots of repetitious paper work isn't the answer. Doing more (quantity) doesn't replace doing something well (quality). Assess and evaluate every technique you use. Make changes (tweaking existing techniques), abandon techniques that aren't working, and try new techniques or ones you have tried previously with the same student.

- You can't be all things to all people (students). Do try to give more time to the weaker students, but don't ignore the stronger students. Stronger students will require modified programs but with less supervision. Instructions to better students can often be done in written form or with a quick example. Another technique is to teach one of the stronger students how to do something and he/she in turn teaches the others.

- Look for Kaizen (the concept of continuous improvement), not just specific targets especially for weaker students. Make sure all students understand and focus on continuous improvement as a realistic way of reaching educational goals. Teaching Kaizen as an attitude or life skill is a worthy objective. At every opportunity point out continuous improvements by individuals and the class. Have students recognize continuous improvement in themselves and their fellow students.

- Parents and students will appreciate anything you can do that is related to individualizing/differentiating instruction. Because you have a plan and a process, you will be able to justify the actions you have taken. Keep accurate records of the progress made. Celebrate even the smallest successes.

**Work Smarter Not Harder**

In order to work smarter not harder in reaching your goals for individualizing and differentiating instruction, consider the following:

- That more than one way of doing things may have to be used to get the desired results. Expand your "bag of tricks" using the techniques you have in this report and adding ones of your own.

- That you may be successful by returning to some methods of instruction you have previously used with the class or with individual students. Recycle your "bag of tricks". As change occurs, an instructional method already tried may work this time.

- That Kaizen (continuous improvement) is a more realistic goal than a specific mark, grade, or percentage.

- That a change in "attitude" is as worthy a goal to eventually lead to academic success as anything else. This applies equally to the teacher and the students. Acceptance of reality, setting realistic goals, reducing frustration, and celebrating small successes are important.

- That you can reduce your stress through goals, objectives, action plans, and by establishing rules and routines. In other words, planning and organization. Starting a year or term with a plan is the best approach.

- That you must put things in perspective and set priorities. You have a prescribed timeline to your school year and a limited amount of energy to make the changes you want to make and accomplish the goals you have set for yourself and your students.

- That Plato's "Know Thyself" works for teachers to know their strengths and make use of them. At the same time, you should be "teaching" students to recognize their strengths and build on these.

- That it takes a team to teach a child and collaboration is the glue that holds the team together. Engage everyone and anyone who has a stake in the individual student's progress at school.

- That the more the teacher understands how the brain works for effective teaching and learning, the more success that teacher will have with the students' progress and success. Keep abreast of the research that is available to you through professional magazines and other sources.

## Strategies for Individualized and Differentiated Instruction

The following are suggested methods of individualizing or differentiating instruction for individual students. You are encouraged to add to this list, modify the suggestions, personalize your approaches, or do whatever works! If you can add to this list, please contact the author, Paul Jackson, so he can update this list. Share your successes as well. That would really be appreciated.

The following descriptions are brief outlines of possible strategies. They are not intended to be prescriptive. It is assumed that as a classroom teacher you can take the idea, do further research if needed, and find a way to introduce the strategy into your classroom.

You will see from the list that I have taken the broadest definition of individualized/differentiated instruction and included techniques that "buy time" for the teacher to work with those who need his/her help the most. There is nothing wrong with that. You are doing it now. Just do it with a little more forethought and planning. It's a reality of classroom life.

## 1. Differentiated Expectations—One Assignment

When creating seatwork, homework, or assignment outlines, put a wide range of options on the sheet to accommodate the range of student abilities from weak to strong. This eliminates creating several different assignments for each of your groups. By doing this, you now have the option with one assignment sheet to assign different questions to different groups of students. You can make some parts mandatory for all students. You can give a specific group of questions to a specific group of students. You can individualize the assignment to just one student if needed. You can use some of the questions as "bonus" questions for different groups. Encourage students to try questions not assigned to them that are more difficult without penalizing them. You can encourage some individuals to try a specific question that may not count on the "test" unless they do well on it. This is helping students reach a little beyond their grasp. You also help students realize the differences from the easier more basic questions and the more difficult ones as well as the questions in between the two extremes. You eliminate having to mark the easier questions of those students for whom they are just too easy. There are a tremendous number of advantages to this approach while reducing work load and saving time. Your marking scheme can reflect the level of difficulty of the questions done and number of questions completed. You can reward effort.

## 2. Pre-test

By giving your students a pre-test, you have the kind of data that takes the guesswork out of making your groups. This also gives students the opportunity to determine which group they belong to. You can modify your teaching strategies for the entire class based on the results. Students will also be able to see themselves as progressing as measured against the pre-test. The responsibility of where the student starts in the unit is determined by the student's ability, as indicated on the pre-test. It is not an arbitrary decision by the teacher. Too little pre-testing is done. It needn't be time consuming. Just ask the basic questions that will separate the groups by ability. Base your individualized instruction on the test results.

### 3. "Cheat-sheets" for the student groups

Providing a "cheat-sheet" of detailed instructions for a unit of study or a mathematics topic or a writing assignment is a good idea. These instructions are your basic teaching outline simplified so students can understand them. You can use this kind of detailed step-by-step method of working through the material for your stronger group who may be able to follow the instructions with little or no help. For the middle-ability groups, the "cheat-sheet" can be something to refer to if they are having problems, fall behind, or want to work ahead. For weaker students, you may have a modified version or not have one at all. These students will likely require most of the help you can give.

### 4. Whole—Part—Whole

One strategy teachers know works is the whole-part-whole approach. You outline the entire "big picture" of what is being taught, break that down into smaller chunks and teach them, and then return to the summary "whole" again to bring it all together. The overview to start with is a way to check for understanding. By asking key questions, you get an understanding of how well the class and the individual students understand the topic. Modify the "parts" to coincide with the understanding. Have students tackle those "parts" they feel capable of handling without direct supervision. You may wish to list the parts in order of difficulty. By outlining them, you are also providing the students with a list of things they must know. It is possible you may be able to eliminate some topics. The summary "whole" may well become your assessment tool.

### 5. Teach to the Test

There is nothing wrong with giving the students the final exam (assessment instrument) at the beginning of the unit. You can even use a modified version of this test as a pre-test. Then teach the students only what is needed to do the test. This applies to teaching students "skills" as well. You can quickly find out where the students stand with some simple examples. This also allows students to determine for themselves which kinds of questions or skills they need to work on. Have students choose one or two that they can readily handle rather than trying to get to them to learn everything they "should" know, but realistically are going to accomplish at this time.

## 6. Give Part Marks

The days should be long gone where you give students an "all or nothing" mark for any question or assignment. Encourage students to show all their work in arriving at their answer. Give students credit for getting part of the question right or attempting the answer. This also gives the teacher some insight into what the student is thinking. Some response is better than no response. Part of the problem of treating students as individuals is getting them to keep doing something. Stronger students often do their thinking without recording anything as to how they arrived at their answer. Emphasize the value of explaining how the answer was created. Use the insights you get to individualize the instruction possibly grouping together those students who are having the same problems.

## 7. Grouping by Ability or Skill Level

Whether your groups are formally or informally put together, it will be obvious to all the students that they are in ability or capability groups. The students KNOW! Don't try to hide it. Students should understand why the groups are they way they are and why it is important from the teacher's point of view to group students. Grouping is a form of individualized instruction and teachers/students should understand that. Even in a mixed ability group, the weaker students benefit from the teaching of the stronger ones and the stronger ones benefit by teaching the weaker ones. The group should show continuous improvement. Find a way to measure improvement in the groups as a whole as well as individuals within the groups.

## 8. Teach to Minimum Objectives

Share with students the minimum objectives or goals that you wish them to achieve and then teach to those objectives. Keep working with the students to reach those objectives. Once those goals are reached, celebrate and move ahead. The students will feel successful and so will the teacher.

Have different goals and objectives for every single student or group of students and communicate them. Individualization can sometimes be as simple as setting realistic goals for each student. Students, in general, should accept the fact that everyone is unique and all students deserve to succeed at his/her own level and rate. Teaching to a minimum objective as the initial target will assure students of a passing grade if they can reach that objective. Of course, most students will go beyond that minimum.

## 9. Quality vs. Quantity

How often are students who already know how to do something asked to keep doing it for "practice" when they don't need to practice? Sometimes this is called busywork. Consider the concept of quality vs. quantity as it applies to individualizing the instruction. Quality should always be the objective, not quantity. Students need to do enough repetition to solidify the learning and no more. You can individualize instruction using the quality vs quantity concept. Students who have mastered a concept need to move on. Students who naturally work slower should be accommodated. Just because some students can do more work doesn't measure mastery of the concepts. Weaker students often benefit from having to do less work with more success.

## 10. Use Student Tutors

You can help individualize instruction using student tutors. These tutors don't necessarily have to come only from your strongest students. Pick students who work and communicate well with others. Train students to help others. Establish guidelines or some do's and don'ts about giving assistance. The tutor's job is keep the student requesting help "moving ahead", not doing the work for her/him. Recognize that tutors are used only when the teacher isn't available. The tutor helps clarify instructions or helps with the next step. Tutors make a student's individualized assistance readily available. Inform the parents of tutors about their role assuring the parents that the program won't interfere with the tutor's schooling. Create an atmosphere in your classroom of teaching and learning not just learning. Students are both teachers and learners.

## 11. Students Marking Students

It is possible for students to assess their own work or another student's work at any grade level. What the student needs to assess their own or someone else's work is a list of specific things to look for that measures mastery. The addition of a rubric that groups these "look-fors" can provide an evaluation system as well. Students can often do the assessment of the look-fors and the teacher can use that to do the evaluation. When students are given the opportunity to assess their own work, they can also be given the opportunity to improve their work because they know exactly what they need to do to improve their assessment. This encourages the student to do "just a little more" to get a better assessment. This works at all ability levels. It instills in students the concept of exceeding expectations. There is nothing wrong with allowing students to go back to their work and do much more than they originally did to better their mark. One thing you must do is start the assessment of work done as early as possible in longer projects. If you wait until the end product is submitted, it is usually too late to capture the "teachable moment" or to help with skill development. Catch students who could benefit from doing just a little more while they can do something about it.

## 12. Volunteers

There are many volunteers you can use in your classroom. They may include other teachers, educational assistants, parent volunteers, high school or college students, or older students in the school. Volunteers allow for individualized instruction with one or two students at a time. The key here is to be well-organized so the goal for each volunteer session is specific within an overall plan for the student. You must minimize the teacher's involvement and maximize the learning experience for the student(s). Make sure the students understand what the volunteer is trying to do and why.

## 13. Use Bonus Incentives

Bonus marks or assignments can be a tremendous incentive to all students at all ability levels. If you do offer a bonus, make certain that you use those marks. Don't just say it's a bonus and then do nothing with the bonus mark. Give real bonuses. Show those bonuses in the final assessment. The objective of the bonus for individualized instruction is that you are then "stretching" the limits of everyone. Don't make the bonuses too onerous or too much work. Give a choice of bonuses based on the ability levels of your students. Offer suggestions for individual students that will focus on a goal for that student. Don't allow the stronger students to take the easy road using a bonus choice that is "beneath" them. Students know when they are doing this. Never punish anyone for not doing a bonus. Stick to positive encouragement.

## 14. Ask students how you are individualizing their program

Have you ever taken the time to ask the students what they might like to do to help them become a better student? Student feedback on the extra help they are getting, the kind of enrichment activities they are doing, the quantity of work they are being asked to do, or any other special attention they may be getting would be invaluable in setting goals and preparing action plans for the future. You will be surprised at how intuitive and honest they can be. They can feel some kind of ownership in their own program. They will all see themselves as having individualized programs. You can answer their questions and explain your point of view.

## 15. Goals and Work/Study Habits

Never assume that students know what to do when you give them something to do. Have them demonstrate they understand what you just taught before they start doing the practice exercises. Teach good student work habits and study habits as you teach the material. Insist on them using what you taught as they do their work. Help students realize the importance of goals and realize that goals are personal. One size does not fit all. When students have individualized goals, they are more likely to succeed. If every student knows what they have to work on during the school year, during the term, and during the unit of study, they are more likely to succeed and you will have individualized their program.

## 16. Train-the-Trainer Technique

A Train-the-Trainer method of sharing knowledge is very effective. It involves selecting a few individuals who are trained in how and what to share with others. Once they master these skills, they share that information with others following a prescribed program. You can use this in the classroom by choosing a few students, teaching them what you want the others in their group to learn, and then giving them the opportunity to "teach" the others. By breaking down the content into manageable chunks, several students can be responsible for sharing the information. It shouldn't always be the same students or the best students. This technique allows the teacher to work with one or two groups or individuals while the other "teachers" are doing their jobs. This doesn't work for every topic, but it can be effective.

## 17. Provide the Answer Sheet

In some subject areas, you can provide students with the correct answers to the work they are doing. This works particularly well in mathematics or anything where there is a right or wrong answer. The purpose here is to allow students to check their own work so they don't do a lot of questions incorrectly before getting the help they may need. Students are taught to get help as soon as they need it. Another idea along the same lines is to provide the correct answers to the exercises on the blackboard or some other display, but put them up in random order. This way, students can check to see if the answer they got is among the correct ones. If yes, move on. If not, try again. If the answer still can't be found, seek help. You get the picture. You must, of course, establish the guidelines so that students realize that the answers are there to help them, not just to copy them down and "pretend" they know what they are doing. This technique works well with 99% of the students, so try it! This places most of the responsibility on the students to work through the correct answers and individualizes the help they need when they need it.

## 18. Enrichment for All

One kind of individualized instruction is to provide enrichment activities for all students. Typically, we think of enrichment for only the stronger students. But if you organize your units of study in such a way as to teach to minimal objectives and leave yourself time at the end for additional activities, you can build enrichment into the program for everyone. The students who usually require additional individualized support can be given enrichment activities as well as the stronger students. Give students a choice of activities. Guide some students to specific activities. Allow others to choose. Regardless of what they choose, set expectations that match the ability levels of individual students. Using the term "enrichment" works wonders with students and using the term in the way you are presenting it is legitimate. You have covered the basics of the unit and can now enrich it.

# SETTING AND ACHIEVING YOUR GOALS WITH S.U.C.C.E.S.S.

*Marjan Glavac*

## Why Have Goals?

**If you do not know where you are going, any road will take you there.**
*—The Cheshire Cat, Alice In Wonderland.*

**A journey of a thousand miles, begins with the first step.**
*—Chinese proverb*

**Clear measurable goals are the centre to the mystery of a school's success, mediocrity, or failure.**
*—Rosenholtz, S. J.*

*The introduction of specific, measurable goals is among the most promising yet underused strategies we can introduce into school improvement efforts.*
*—Mike Schmoker*

**Select substantive slices Ц small but meaningful challenges that promote success and hence optimism.**
*—Mike Schmoker*

**Some Truths about Time and Goal Setting**

1. Each of us receives twenty-four hours a day, or 1,440 minutes, or 86,400 seconds. Every day we're given the same amount of time. When we decide to spend the time, we're deciding to not spend it on something else.

2. You can only control the time you have right now. You cannot alter the past, you cannot control the future.

3. You don't have to do everything alone. Two heads are better than one.

4. There is more than one way to do something.

6. Setting goals will give you more time. Planning puts you in control.

If you're not determined to change, you will not have control over your time. Things will only change in your class when you decide to change. If you don't do anything to change, they'll stay the same or get worse. Time management and goal setting are really about change and control. You want to be able to control your time. The more control you have, the less stress you have, the better you feel. Andrew Carnegie summarized this in the following quote:

**"If you want to be happy, set a goal that commands your thoughts, liberates your energy, and inspires your hopes".**

Once you have a goal, you get to say *no* to everything else. A goal reflects your personality, your philosophy, and your values. When you set a goal, you are deciding what's important to you. It forces you to look at something that you're lacking and make it better. It sharpens your focus. It gives you control over the things that you think are most important to you. The time, effort, and resources you decide to spend on your goal are resources that aren't spent on anything else. It gives a direction to your most valuable and precious resource—time. Goals shape who you want to become.

Goals force you to do something different, something outside your comfort zone. There is a possibility that you might fail. This is the risk you assume when you take on a goal. But once your goals are achieved, you will become a better person. You will increase your learning, acquire new skills, and build up your self-confidence. You will also build up new experiences that you can call upon when facing new challenges.

Your goals need to be important to you. They need to have value for you. They need to come from deep inside of you. You will achieve them if you are committed and determined to do it.

# The Goal Setting Process, or How to Do It

**Where Do Goals Come From?**

Areas for you to consider when choosing your goals:

Career

Community

Financial

Hobbies

Mental Health

Physical Health

Personal Relationships

Professional Relationships

Academic/Intellectual

Spiritual Development

To help you narrow down this list, here's a list of values that was generated by a nationwide survey by the Franklin Quest Company:

1. Spouse
2. Financial security
3. Personal health and fitness
4. Children and Family
5. Spirituality/Religion
6. A sense of accomplishment
7. Integrity and Honesty
8. Occupational satisfaction
9. Love for others/Service

10. Education and Learning
11. Self-respect
12. Taking responsibility
13. Exercising leadership
14. Inner harmony
15. Independence
16. Intelligence and Wisdom
17. Understanding
18. Quality of life
19. Happiness/Positive attitude
20. Pleasure
21. Self-control
22. Ambition
23. Being capable
24. Imagination and Creativity
25. Forgiveness
26. Generosity
27. Equality
28. Friendship
29. Beauty
30. Courage

## Characteristics of Effective Goal Setting

Effective goal setting can be summarized by the acronym **SUCCESS:**

**S**pecific

**U**nderstand your Why

**C**hallenge Yourself

Consider and Clear the Obstacles

Encourage Yourself

Stay Focused

Show Your Success

## Specific

Goals need to be specific and measurable. They need to be written down. An unwritten goal is just a wish, a desire. Writing is the doing part of thinking.

When writing down your goal, be as specific as you can. For example, saying "I want all my students to be able to read" is too vague of a goal. Writing "by October 20th, all of my students will have read two passages of text out loud to me" is much more specific and measurable goal. "I am going to lose weight" is just a wish; "I am going to lose three pounds by January 31st at 8:00 a.m." is more purposeful. The more you can focus, target, and measure your goal, the more it will be successful.

Our minds are hardwired to work towards a deadline. Ever wonder why contract negotiations heat up when the deadline looms ever nearer? Why sports teams pour on the extra efforts in the last minutes and seconds of the game? Why a lot of students ask for an extension just before an assignment is due? When you set a time to get something done, your mind will be motivated to meet that deadline. There is a sense of urgency, a reason to take action. With no time limit, there is no leverage, no real reason to get anything done or to even start.

## Understand Your Why

Have a reason why you are doing the goal. It needs a valid purpose. Make sure it's your own goal and not someone else's. Answer the question, "why do I want this?" as passionately and enthusiastically as you can. The bigger the why, the bigger the connection, the more you will want to achieve the goal. To help you find your "why", look over the areas discussed earlier when choosing your goals and your values. Aligning your goals with your values will strengthen their purpose and ensure success.

If you still have difficulty deciding on a goal, look over the areas and values and decide what you don't want. Years ago, one of my lowest priorities was being in good physical shape. Now, it is one of my top goals.

Another strategy to use to decide on your "why" is to consider what will happen when your goal is completed. What are the benefits, the payoffs, the advantages to you once your goal is completed? How will you become a better person once your goal is accomplished?

For my goal of being in good physical shape, I thought of all the health benefits, the improvement to my mind and well-being, the ability to go up stairs without being winded, and the extra energy I'd have.

Think as well about all the disadvantages you will face if the goal is not completed. What are the negatives of not getting it done? The more pain you can associate with not getting the goal achieved, the more you will be motivated to getting it done. Not being in physical shape, to me, meant the possibility of illness, medical bills, a lack of energy, and not being able to participate in physical activities with my students, family, and friends. This realization of the pain involved if I didn't get in shape motivated me to go to the gym and do my exercises even when I was more motivated to sleep in and put it off for another day.

## Challenge Yourself

Challenge yourself by choosing a goal that will make you grow and stretch as a person. Challenge yourself to go beyond what you once did. You'll grow more as a person when you go outside your comfort zone.

Early in my teaching career, I made a decision to leave the comfort of teaching French to students in Grades Four, Five, and Six. I took on the challenge of teaching French and Science to a self-contained Grade Seven Special Education class, two periods of Language Arts and French to another Grade Seven class, French to a Grade Eight class, and French to a Grade Six class. Although it was a challenge, the skills I learned helped me when I became a resource teacher and when I had my own homeroom class.

By challenging yourself, you become a role model for others. If you can do it, others can. Consider the achievement of Roger Bannister. For years, it was thought impossible to run a mile in under four minutes. Within weeks of Bannister accomplishing his goal on May 6th, 1954, he inspired others to run the mile in under four minutes. In fact, he was so successful that he held the record for the least amount of time! On breaking the four-minute mile, Roger Bannister was quoted as saying, "No longer conscious of my movement, I discovered a new unity with nature. I had found a new source of power and beauty, a source I never dreamt existed."

Now *that's* stretching and challenging yourself!

## Consider and Clear the Obstacles

Don't set yourself up for failure by setting too many goals or goals that have too many obstacles to overcome. There are goals that will cause you more pain than they're worth. Avoid these. Aim for one to three manageable goals. Remember that you can't do it all. Change is incremental and is achieved in small steps.

**Inch by inch, it's a cinch. Mile by mile, it's a trial.**

Realistically, I will never be good enough to be a professional musician, artist, or athlete. I can improve myself in those areas, but for me to compete with professionals, who have spent their entire lives perfecting their craft, is unrealistic.

In school, having a student read at a Grade Eight level by the end of the school year is unreasonable and unrealistic if he's presently only reading at a Grade Three level, is absent from school for a majority of the time, and lacks parental support. To make it more reasonable and achievable, consider the obstacles preventing him from attaining the goal. Clear those obstacles away and make the goal more reasonable. A goal of increasing the student's attendance at school clears an obstacle. If he's at school more often, there'll be a better chance to have him spend more time on task for reading.

Consider the obstacles that need to be overcome for you to succeed. There will be setbacks. There will be times when you don't want to work on achieving your goal. It's okay to have a "day off". It's okay to fine-tune your actions. Treat these obstacles as minor speed bumps and not roadblocks on your journey to success.

Use the salami or Swiss cheese technique to clear your obstacles. Instead of being overwhelmed by a challenging task, break it down. Take thin slices of the task, like slicing a salami, until it's done; or poke enough holes in it until it's done like Swiss cheese. By consistently spending as little as fifteen minutes a day on your obstacle, it will soon be cleared away.

## Encourage Yourself

A quick way to successful completion of your goal is to have people who can help and encourage you. These may be coaches, mentors, friends, teams, networks, or mastermind groups.

By working with others, you're now making your goals known to other people. Your goals now become more publicly known.

By making it public and by putting it out there, you now become more accountable for your goal to yourself and to others.

This is a very powerful motivator. Knowing that there are others encouraging you, helping you, and cheering you on will motivate you to go on when you become discouraged.

You will accomplish much more working with others than working by yourself. The energy of a group working together as a team will create breakthroughs for you. They will challenge you. They will move you out of your comfort zone and out of your old routines and habits. They will help you to brainstorm for ideas, connect you with other like-minded people, and give you valuable feedback. You will learn faster, gain years of experience quicker, and avoid "reinventing the wheel". Results will come faster. You will find newer ways of doing things, come up with better ideas, and "think outside the box". It will develop a sense of not wanting to let people down. Of not giving up.

There are many reasons why successful athletes, executives, actors, singers, and dancers have coaches, mentors, friends, teams, networks, or mastermind groups. It's because they work! You need their thoughts, feelings, and actions to help encourage you to accomplish your goal.

As a teacher, working with a colleague or a team helps to break the isolation of the classroom and minimizes burnout by sharing success stories and strategies that work. They offer a safe opportunity to vent your frustration with someone who's been there. Younger teachers benefit from experienced teachers. Experienced teachers benefit from younger teachers. Teacher collaboration and teamwork can offer new ideas on different teaching methods, newer technology, and innovative ways of looking at challenges in the classroom. Resources can be more easily identified and shared. You'll work smarter, not harder, by working with others.

## Stay Focused

Clearing away distractions, setting aside time, and consistently reviewing your goal will produce results. Stay focused by having an action plan and practice it daily.

One action plan to stay focused is to review your goal at least 3 times a day. You can do this by having your goal written down on an index card and reading it just after you get up in the morning, at noontime and just before going to sleep.

Another way is by doing a visualization exercise. Schedule 5–10 minutes in a place you can go to daily that is free of distractions. Sit in a chair and make yourself comfortable. Close your eyes and visualize your goal. Make a movie in your mind. See yourself in the movie working towards your goal. Think about times in your life when you experienced a positive emotion such as past success. It may be the time got you placed first in a competition, delivered your first public speech, had a role in a play, played in a band, received your degree, got your first car, house, got married, witnessed the birth of your child, went on your dream trip. Take that positive emotion and connect that feeling with your goal. Create a positive mental picture of your goal by making it as real as possible. Visualizing it using all your senses. Listen and think how your goal tastes like, feels like, sounds like and smells like. Make it as real as possible. Your goal needs to be acted upon with certainty that you will not fail.

When I was learning French at university, I labeled everything in my room in French. I listened to French tapes, went to the language laboratory to practice speaking it and joined French clubs to interact with native speakers. I ate French cuisine and learned French cooking. I immersed myself in the language and culture by taking summer courses in Quebec and living with French speaking families. I later visited French speaking countries such as France, Belgium and Switzerland to practice my French in real life situations. When I returned from Europe I studied to become an elementary French teacher.

When your goal becomes the first thing you consistently think about before you begin your day and the last thing you consistently think about before you go to sleep, it will become imprinted in your mind. It will become a part of you. You will have effectively rewired your brain to think about your goal in a positive, constructive way. You will be training your brain to go out and seek connections to accomplish your goal. Every time you come across something to do about your goal, your brain will focus on it.

## Show Your Success

You've done it! You've achieved your goal. Tell the world what you've accomplished. Although it's hard for a lot of us to "toot our own horns", I'm reminded of a quote by baseball pitcher Dizzy Dean "It ain't bragging if you can back it up."

Be proud of your accomplishment. If you haven't done so, take your past diplomas and awards and proudly display them in your classroom. If my mechanic, doctor, lawyer, and dentist can display their diplomas and awards in their offices, teachers should too.

Announce your accomplishment in your school, teacher, district, community and university newsletters. Send out an email to your closest friends, your coaches, teams, mentors. Include it in your annual Christmas or New Year's letter to relatives and friends.

You rightly deserve all the recognition and rewards for your accomplishment. Celebrate your achievement. Remember this feeling of accomplishment, for no one can take it away from you.

# 2 Handouts—one for teachers, and one for students.

**Handout**—example of a goal setting sheet for teachers:

## Teacher Goal Setting Template

Teaching Goal

School Goal

Personal Goal

Professional Development

Extra-Curricular Activity

Resources Required

1. _______________________________________

2. _______________________________________

3. _______________________________________

4. _______________________________________

What is my goal? Be as specific as possible.

_______________________________________

_______________________________________

_______________________________________

Why do I want this goal?

1. _______________________________________

2. _______________________________________

3. _______________________________________

## How will this goal challenge me?

1. _______________________________________

2. _______________________________________

3. _______________________________________

## What are the obstacles?

1. _______________________________________

2. _______________________________________

3. _______________________________________

## Who will encourage me to accomplish my goal?

1. _______________________________________

2. _______________________________________

3. _______________________________________

## How will I stay focused on my goal?

1. _______________________________________

2. _______________________________________

3. _______________________________________

## How will I show my success?

1. _______________________________________

2. _______________________________________

3. _______________________________________

**Handout**—example of a goal setting sheet for students:

Name _______________

Date _______________

# Monthly goal

My goal is: _______________________________________

Steps
To reach my goal, I plan to take these steps:

    1. _______________________________

    2. _______________________________

    3. _______________________________

Helpers
These are people who can help me:

    1. _______________________________

    2. _______________________________

    3. _______________________________

Obstacles
I must watch out for:

    1. _______________________________

    2. _______________________________

    3. _______________________________

Time Line
I plan to achieve this goal by:

_______________________________________

Reward
My reward for successfully achieving this goal will be:

_______________________________________

_______________________________________

## Values

| | | |
|---|---|---|
| Acceptance | Accessibility | Accomplishment Accuracy |
| Advancement and promotion | Adventure | Abundance |
| Affection | Altruism | Ambition |
| Appreciation | Approachability | Arts |
| Assertiveness | Assurance | Attentiveness Attractiveness |
| Autonomy | Balance | Beauty |
| Belonging | Boldness | Bravery |
| Calmness | Camaraderie | Candor |
| Career Success | Caring | Challenge |
| Change | Cheerfulness | Clarity |
| Cleanliness | Close Relationships | Collaboration |
| Comfort | Commitment | Communication |
| Community | Compassion | Competence |
| Competition | Concentration | Confidence |
| Conformity | Congruency | Consistency |
| Contentment | Continuous improvement | Contribution |
| Control | Conviction | Coolness |
| Courage | Courtesy | Creativity |
| Credibility | Curiosity | Decisiveness |
| Decorum | Democracy | Dedication |
| Determination | Devotion | Dignity |
| Diligence | Discipline | Discovery |
| Discretion | Diversity | Dress |
| Duty | Eagerness | Ease of Use |
| Ecology | Economic Security | Education |
| Efficiency | Elegance | Empathy |
| Encouragement | Endurance | Enjoyment |
| Entertainment | Ethics | Enthusiasm |
| Equality | Ethnic roots | Excellence |
| Excitement | Experience | Expertise |
| Expressiveness | Fairness | Faith |

| | | |
|---|---|---|
| Fame | Family | Fashion |
| Fidelity | Firmness | Fitness |
| Flexibility | Focus | Freedom |
| Friendliness | Friendship | Frugality |
| Fun | Generosity | Gratitude |
| Growth | Globalism | Good will |
| Happiness | Hard work | Harmony |
| Health | Helpfulness | Heroism |
| Honesty | Honor | Hopefulness |
| Hospitality | Humility | Humor |
| Hygiene | Impartiality | Individualism |
| Independence | Influencing others | Ingenuity |
| Inner peace | Inspiration | Integrity |
| Intelligence | Intimacy | Intuition |
| Innovation | Investing | Involvement |
| Job tranquility | Joy | Justice |
| Kindness | Knowledge | Law Abiding |
| Leadership | Learning | Linguistic |
| Logic | Love | Loyalty |
| Making a difference | Marital Harmony | Mastery |
| Maturity | Meaning | Mentoring Others |
| Merit | Modesty | Money |
| Morality | Motivation | Music |
| Mysteriousness | Nature | Neatness |
| Obedience | Open-mindedness | Openness |
| Optimism | Order | Orderly Home Life |
| Organization | Originality | Passion |
| Patriotism | Peace | Perceptiveness |
| Perfection | Persistence | Personal Growth |
| Persuasiveness | Philanthropy | Physical challenge |
| Pleasantness | Pleasure | Popularity |
| Positive Mental Attitude | Reasonableness | Recognition |

| | | |
|---|---|---|
| Recreation | Reflection | Relationships |
| Relaxation | Reliability | Religion |
| Reputation | Resilience | Resolve |
| Resourcefulness | Respect | Responsibility |
| Rest | Restraint | Results-oriented |
| Reverence | Rule of Law | Sacrifice |
| Safety | Satisfaction | Security |
| Self-control | Selflessness | Self-reliance |
| Sensitivity | Sensuality | Serenity |
| Service | Sexuality | Sharing |
| Shrewdness | Significance | Silence |
| Simplicity | Sincerity | Skill |
| Solidarity | Solitude | Speed |
| Spirituality | Spontaneity | Stability |
| Power | Practicality | Preparedness |
| Preservation | Privacy | Proactive |
| Problem Solving | Professionalism | Progress |
| Prosperity | Public service | Punctuality |
| Standardization | Status | Strength |
| Structure | Success | Support |
| Surprise | Sympathy | Synergy |
| Teamwork | Thankfulness | Thoughtfulness |
| Thrift | Time | Tolerance of Others |
| Tradition | Tranquility | Trust |
| Truth | Understanding | Uniqueness |
| Unity | Usefulness | Variety |
| Vigor | Virtue | Vision |
| Vitality | Volunteerism | Warmth |
| Wealth | Willingness | Winning |
| Wisdom | Wittiness | Wonder |
| Working alone | Working under pressure | Working with others |
| Youthfulness | Zeal | |

# ASSESSMENT AND EVALUATION

## Assessment and Evaluation
## What Is The Big Difference?

*Marjan Glavac*

"In this era of heightened interest in school reform, we have yet to realize that organizations typically get what they earnestly and specifically set out to get. Good faith efforts to establish goals and then to collectively and regularly monitor and adjust actions toward them produce results."

—*Dr. Mike Schmoker*

"If we expect students to do excellent work, they have to know what excellent work looks like"

—*Dr. Grant Wiggins*

"Students can hit any target they can see and that doesn't move."

—*Dr. Richard Stiggins*

### Presumptions: Assessment and Evaluation

The primary purpose of assessment and evaluation is to improve student learning. Information gathered through assessment helps teachers to determine students' strengths and weaknesses in their achievement of the curriculum expectations in each course. This information also serves to guide teachers in adapting curriculum and instructional approaches to students' needs and in assessing the overall effectiveness of programs and classroom practices.

The terms assessment and evaluation are interrelated but not synonymous. Assessment precedes evaluation.

Assessment is the data you collect about what students know, are able to do, and are working toward in order to arrive at a final evaluation. Assessment is objective data collection. It includes a variety of techniques for collecting data which is then compiled for future reference. It is the marking of the work, the tests and assignments that are done and graded or turned in for marks. Assessment methods and tools include: observation, student self-assessments, daily practice assignments, quizzes, samples of student work, pencil-and-paper tests, holistic rating scales, projects, oral and written reports, performance reviews, and portfolio assessments.

Evaluation is the interpretation of the assessment data. Student performance is evaluated from the information collected through assessment activities. It involves judgement against selected criteria based on relevant data. It is a more subjective decision based on the assessment. The more extensive and comprehensive the data, the more accurate will be the evaluation. Evaluation is the overall final "mark". Teachers use their insight, knowledge about learning, and experience with students, along with the specific criteria they establish, to make judgments about student performance in relation to prescribed learning outcomes.

It is the summative mark for the report card or the final mark in a project that may have had several parts that were assessed. Evaluations are done using multiple assessments. It is an important distinction.

Students benefit most when evaluation is provided on a regular, ongoing basis. When evaluation is seen as an opportunity to promote learning rather than as a final judgment, it shows learners their strengths and suggests how they can develop further.

Students can use this information to redirect efforts, make plans, and establish future learning goals.

For this survey the focus is on assessment and the related collection of data. As part of the formative process of evaluation of instruction in the classroom it is especially relevant. Good teaching will incorporate a variety of assessment methods to ensure an accurate evaluation.

**Teacher Use of the Survey**

This survey can be used for self-evaluation by the teacher. It addresses the issues of assessment devices, assessment methods, and the beliefs of the teacher about assessment. The survey results are intended to stimulate reflective thought. The survey will give an idea of the presently used methods and current beliefs of the teacher. It is not intended to be an evaluation of the teacher's assessment techniques but rather an inventory of presently used methods. It may foster professional growth by reminding the teacher of methods not being used at the present time and methods not previously used by the classroom teacher.

**Explanation of the terms in the survey**

**Assessment Devices** are defined as the hands-on things that you use to collect the data. These are the concrete products of the data collection not the methods by which the information was collected. You may define devices as the collection agencies for the data, the things you can take with you to a meeting about the student.

**Assessment Methods** are defined as the techniques, processes or methods used to gather the data to be placed in the assessment devices. The methods are the "doing" part of the assessment process. It is here where the number and variety of the methods is paramount. The greater the variety the more likelihood there is that each student's evaluation will accurately reflect his-her abilities relative to the selected criteria. The data collected must be free of bias and objective in nature. It is here also where the teacher's creativity and sensitivity play a major role for some students. Since one of the purposes of evaluation is to set future goals for students it is also important that progress toward those goals be measured against the data collected in the past. Accuracy and clarity are important.

**Assessment Beliefs** are defined as the attitudes and educational philosophies behind the actions taken by the classroom teacher. At times they may be confused with the methods of assessment. The distinction between methods and beliefs does not warrant a great deal of debate. They are interrelated. What is important though is to have the teacher examine his-her belief system in order to assess past performance and set future goals

## Assessment and Evaluation Survey

Please rate the following assessment devices, methods and beliefs according to the frequency of their use in your classroom. These surveys are a snapshot of the present situation. Repetition of the survey periodically is necessary. Spaces are provided for write-ins. These surveys are designed as a process for "reflection" leading to change.

| ASSESSMENT DEVICES | Never | Seldom | Sometimes | Usually | Always | Not Applicable |
|---|---|---|---|---|---|---|
| Examinations | | | | | | |
| Tests | | | | | | |
| Projects | | | | | | |
| School Records | | | | | | |
| Recording Keeping—Marks Book | | | | | | |
| Student Work Folder | | | | | | |
| Standardized Tests | | | | | | |
| Student Profiles | | | | | | |
| Minutes of Meetings with Stakeholders | | | | | | |
| Student Assessment (Anecdotal) Folder | | | | | | |
| Assignments | | | | | | |
| Writing Folder | | | | | | |
| Reading Folder | | | | | | |
| Mathematics Folder | | | | | | |
| Projects Folder | | | | | | |
| Previous Report Cards | | | | | | |
| Present Report Card | | | | | | |

# How to Thrive and Survive in Your Classroom

## Assessment and Evaluation Survey

Please rate the following assessment devices, methods and beliefs according to the frequency of their use in your classroom. These surveys are a snapshot of the present situation. Repetition of the survey periodically is necessary. Spaces are provided for write-ins. These surveys are designed as a process for "reflection" leading to change.

| ASSESSMENT DEVICES | Never | Seldom | Sometimes | Usually | Always | Not Applicable |
|---|---|---|---|---|---|---|
| **Tests—Examinations** | | | | | | |
| Unit Tests | | | | | | |
| Quickie Tests—Quizzes | | | | | | |
| Oral Tests | | | | | | |
| Open Book Tests | | | | | | |
| Take Home Tests | | | | | | |
| Skills Tests | | | | | | |
| Attitudinal Surveys | | | | | | |
| Group Tests | | | | | | |
| Informal one-on-one Tests | | | | | | |
| **Evaluations** | | | | | | |
| Self evaluations | | | | | | |
| Peer evaluations | | | | | | |
| Teacher evaluations | | | | | | |
| Group Work—Individual evaluations | | | | | | |
| Group Work—Whole Group evaluations | | | | | | |
| **Oral Assessments** | | | | | | |
| Demonstrations, experiments... | | | | | | |
| Speeches—formal | | | | | | |
| Speeches—informal | | | | | | |
| Conferencing | | | | | | |
| Classroom Participation | | | | | | |
| Work in small groups | | | | | | |

## Assessment and Evaluation Survey

Please rate the following assessment devices, methods and beliefs according to the frequency of their use in your classroom. These surveys are a snapshot of the present situation. Repetition of the survey periodically is necessary. Spaces are provided for write-ins. These surveys are designed as a process for "reflection" leading to change.

| ASSESSMENT DEVICES | Never | Seldom | Sometimes | Usually | Always | Not Applicable |
|---|---|---|---|---|---|---|
| **Types of Questions Used** | | | | | | |
| Short Answers | | | | | | |
| Essay | | | | | | |
| Multiple Choice | | | | | | |
| Product—specific information/facts | | | | | | |
| Process—explanatory | | | | | | |
| Opinion | | | | | | |
| Reflective | | | | | | |
| Cloze | | | | | | |
| Fill in the Blanks | | | | | | |
| Matching | | | | | | |
| True-False; Yes-No... | | | | | | |
| Hypothetical | | | | | | |
| Problem-solving | | | | | | |
| **Instructional Groups** | | | | | | |
| Whole Class | | | | | | |
| Small Groups | | | | | | |
| Individualized Instruction | | | | | | |
| Peer Teaching—Coaching | | | | | | |
| Cross Grouping by Ability or Grade | | | | | | |
| **Teacher Observations** | | | | | | |
| Checklists | | | | | | |
| Anecdotal Comments | | | | | | |
| Rating Scales | | | | | | |
| Audio/Visual Recordings | | | | | | |

## Assessment and Evaluation Survey

Please rate the following assessment devices, methods and beliefs according to the frequency of their use in your classroom. These surveys are a snapshot of the present situation. Repetition of the survey periodically is necessary. Spaces are provided for write-ins. These surveys are designed as a process for "reflection" leading to change.

| ASSESSMENT DEVICES | Never | Seldom | Sometimes | Usually | Always | Not Applicable |
|---|---|---|---|---|---|---|
| **Anecdotal Records** | | | | | | |
| Index File Cards | | | | | | |
| Academic Log Book or Journal | | | | | | |
| At a Glance Recording Sheet | | | | | | |
| Diary | | | | | | |
| Conference Log | | | | | | |
| **Marking Methods** | | | | | | |
| Holistic | | | | | | |
| Letter Grades—defined | | | | | | |
| Rubrics | | | | | | |
| Numerical Scores—fractional i.e. 3/5 | | | | | | |
| Percentages | | | | | | |
| Comments/Suggestions for Improvement | | | | | | |
| Predetermined Criteria—e.g. rubrics | | | | | | |
| Testing to the Objectives | | | | | | |
| Marking each progressive step | | | | | | |
| Pre-test and post-test | | | | | | |
| **Miscellaneous Methods of Data Collection** | | | | | | |
| Marking Seatwork | | | | | | |
| Monitoring Homework | | | | | | |
| Notebooks Marked | | | | | | |
| Classroom Participation | | | | | | |
| Use of Academic Contacts with Students | | | | | | |
| Use of Student "Planning" sheets | | | | | | |

## Assessment and Evaluation Survey

Please rate the following assessment devices, methods and beliefs according to the frequency of their use in your classroom. These surveys are a snapshot of the present situation. Repetition of the survey periodically is necessary. Spaces are provided for write-ins. These surveys are designed as a process for "reflection" leading to change.

| ASSESSMENT DEVICES | Never | Seldom | Sometimes | Usually | Always | Not Applicable |
|---|---|---|---|---|---|---|
| Place the marking scheme on all tests/exams | | | | | | |
| Share marking criteria before assignment | | | | | | |
| Provide opportunities for bonus marks | | | | | | |
| Permit re-writes of tests | | | | | | |
| Set deadlines with penalties/rewards | | | | | | |
| Extend due dates on assignments | | | | | | |
| Assign homework on a regular basis | | | | | | |
| Consider ability groups when creating tests | | | | | | |
| Assign questions to students based on ability | | | | | | |
| Guarantee a minimum of success on assignments | | | | | | |
| Share the learning objectives with students | | | | | | |
| Teach to the Objectives | | | | | | |
| Test to the Objectives | | | | | | |
| Write the test yourself before administering it | | | | | | |
| Teach study and review skills | | | | | | |
| Tell students exactly what is to be tested | | | | | | |
| Adjust test results that are too high or low | | | | | | |
| Comment constructively on all work | | | | | | |
| Mark all the work assigned | | | | | | |
| Use test results to evaluate the method of instruction | | | | | | |
| Mark positively—Use no X's only check marks | | | | | | |
| Use red pen or pencil for marking | | | | | | |
| Keep a comment file on each student | | | | | | |
| Allow for individual differences in marking | | | | | | |
| Use ability groups for instruction | | | | | | |
| Send work home for signing/comments by parents | | | | | | |
| Write parent newsletters for their information | | | | | | |
| Employ rewards systems for good work/effort | | | | | | |

## Assessment and Evaluation Survey

Please rate the following assessment devices, methods and beliefs according to the frequency of their use in your classroom. These surveys are a snapshot of the present situation. Repetition of the survey periodically is necessary. Spaces are provided for write-ins. These surveys are designed as a process for "reflection" leading to change.

| ASSESSMENT DEVICES | Never | Seldom | Sometimes | Usually | Always | Not Applicable |
|---|---|---|---|---|---|---|
| Solicit student opinions regarding assessment | | | | | | |
| Create the test before beginning the unit | | | | | | |
| Use pre-tests to determine objectives of unit | | | | | | |
| Use assessments to evaluate teaching strategies | | | | | | |
| Do a self-evaluation after each unit | | | | | | |
| Share ideas about assessment with peers | | | | | | |
| Read or take courses for professional development | | | | | | |
| Believe in using a variety of assessment methods | | | | | | |
| Use diagnostic assessment instruments | | | | | | |
| Reflect on effectiveness of assess. Methods | | | | | | |
| Request parent comments on work sent home | | | | | | |
| Are familiar with recent research on assess. | | | | | | |
| Recognize assess as on on-going process | | | | | | |
| See the need student specific assess. methods | | | | | | |
| Focus on the learner's strengths | | | | | | |
| Encourage risk-taking; demonstrate it | | | | | | |
| Sharing information is seen as valuable | | | | | | |
| Assessment should be non-competitive | | | | | | |
| Set future goals based on past performance | | | | | | |
| Promote self-evaluation and self-monitoring | | | | | | |
| Give the final responsibility to the learner | | | | | | |
| Challenge the student at the appropriate level | | | | | | |
| Program for success | | | | | | |
| Provide remediation when necessary | | | | | | |
| Allow students choices of assess. methods | | | | | | |
| Make connections between effort and outcome | | | | | | |
| Incorporate game-like features in assessment | | | | | | |

## Some Thoughts To Keep In Mind

Parents want to know what their children are actually learning. The goal of education is to accomplish a result or an outcome.

Use assessment as a way of improving your teaching.

Decide on what your students need to know, based on assessment and evaluation, then design meaningful tasks and assessments. Design tasks that are aligned to student learning styles i.e. auditory, visual, tactile, analytic, kinesthetic etc.

Data should drive instruction and student learning. Students need to ask themselves "what resources and tools do I need to accomplish the task" "what are my goals" "how will I get it done" "Who can help me? Teach goal setting.

Assessment and Evaluation is like making constant course corrections on the way to your destination. Without constant course corrections, space missions would completely miss the earth. Your map is your curriculum. Your directions are your lessons. Your signposts are your criteria. Your final destination are the outcomes you want your students to achieve.

While traveling, you're always assessing where you're going. Sometimes you make a wrong turn, you end up on a number of streets and side roads before you finally make it to the open highway. Once you're on the highway, you're constantly adjusting your speed for the traffic. Sometimes you need to slow down, sometimes you want to speed up and pass. And sometimes, there's nothing you can do but wait as traffic backs up in front of you. That's when you turn your attention to the radio, scenery, conversation. Once you finally get to your destination, you evaluate which route was the best, what worked what didn't. You file the experience somewhere in your mind and call on it again the next time you travel.

## Optimize the Assessment Data

To make a difference in our teaching, we need to look at the assessment data. We need to look at this data to see what we are doing that is making a difference.

Based on the level of my students, what can they do?

What do they need to do?

What do I need to do to make a difference?

Once the material has been taught, and assessed, what aspect of my teaching made a difference?

Did students make progress?

How do I know they made progress?

Did students attain unit objectives and outcomes? Why or why not?

What worked, what didn't?

Which lessons, assessments, criteria need to be modified, fine tuned, discarded?

Would I teach this unit again?

Would I teach it differently?

For more ideas, go back and review Effective Methods For Teaching Units Of Study.

# ASSESSMENT AND EVALUATION –THINK RUBRIC

*Paul Jackson*

## Assessment and Evaluation—Think Rubric!

Rubrics that are thoughtfully designed and used are the absolute best method of assessment and evaluation. When personalized to the class and designed by the teacher they save time and enhance the teaching/learning experience of both the teacher and the students. Rubrics should drive your entire program as well as provide the assessment and evaluation tools that measure progress. Rubrics are the "superman" of assessment and evaluation.

### ASSESSMENT versus EVALUATION

Assessment is the collection of objective data on which the evaluation depends using a variety of assessment techniques or strategies.

Evaluation is the summative subjective judgment of a body of work against selected criteria based on relevant data (assessments). The more subjective evaluation component must be justified by the data accumulated in the assessment portion.

One primary difference between assessment and evaluation is the objectivity of the assessment versus the more subjective nature of the evaluation. Even though evaluation is professionally more subjective in nature, it is based on objectively collected assessments.

Both assessment and evaluation are measured against some pre-determined scale. The scale may be a number scale or a word description scale. The scale may be 1, 2, 3, or A, B, C, D or Excellent, Very Good, Fair, Poor or Percentages like 55%, 65%, 75%, 85%. Each of the scales must have the scale point described in more detail in order to differentiate among the choices.

## BACKGROUND INFORMATION

New methods of instruction introduced over the past few years with different objectives, skills development, process over product emphasis, and the measurement of the attitudinal component of learning necessitates new assessment techniques.

There is a need for clearly stated purposes and objectives for work being done by the students. The students need to know before, during and after the completed work exactly what is expected of them by the teacher and by themselves in the form of personal goals.

Students are an integral part of the teaching-learning process in the classroom.

**Education doesn't happen TO students but WITH students.**

The teacher is not omnipotent. Students need to be involved in the assessment process since expectations are communicated through the assessment. Rubrics are excellent for self-assessment. Students can easily compare their work to the standards outlined in the look-fors and accurately predict what mark they would receive. Involve students in the creation of the rubrics. This is a powerful teaching tool as you are establishing the objectives for and with the students. Peer evaluations are the next logical step in the process of self-evaluation. So now you have teacher evaluation, self-evaluation and peer evaluation with the same rubric.

Self-assessment rubrics can be of a generic nature as well. Instead of measuring specific targets based on curriculum you can also measure personal traits and habits. It can be easy to self-assess or self-evaluate on a scale using for example: excellent, good, fair and poor. Students can rate themselves on things such as: effort, work habits, meeting deadlines, doing more than expected…

Assessment strategies "drive" the system from objectives to evaluation. Teachers and students need to know where they are going, what they are presently doing and what they need to do in the future to improve.

Students must be "shown" and "deliberately taught" how to set personal goals, how to attain them, how to evaluate progress and how to transfer knowledge from one situation to another. In other words, **teachers must teach students how to be teachers (with a student body of one!).** This is a valuable life skill.

Teachers require comments, letter grades or marks in order to fulfill the mandate set down by Departments of Education. The marking systems employed by individual teachers must work for the teacher and for the students. The bottom line is assessment and evaluation methods are the most important part of the teaching/learning process only because it is against this assessment and evaluation that students, classes, schools and systems are compared.

The rubric is one such method of assessment and evaluation. It has endless possibilities in the hands and minds of dedicated, creative professionals. By involving students in the design, use and interpretation of rubrics for assessment and evaluation, the teacher is making the learning process specific to each student individually.

The rubric is also a tool that necessitates a more reflective approach to what is going on in classrooms. We can always use more reflection. Reflection is food for the soul!

Keep your rubrics as simple and straight-forward as possible. Avoid confusion. Be succinct in your descriptors. Measure only what you absolutely need to measure and break down complex components into simple ones.

## RUBRIC BASICS

Definition:

A rubric refers to the scoring **form** used to **measure** specific **criteria** to be **judged**.

**Notes:** Rubrics are used to set goals or objectives

Rubrics are used to measure an individual's progress either the student's or the teacher's.

Rubrics are used to compare an individual's work against a standard or benchmark.

Rubrics are used to set future goals by teachers and students.

Rubrics are used to collaboratively set standards of work between the teacher and the student(s).

Rubrics can be used individually, in small groups or in whole class situations.

Rubrics take the "guess work" out of assessment for the students since they know what is being measured and for the teacher because she/he has very specific look-fors that justify the mark or grade given.

Rubrics point out exactly what as accomplished and what was not accomplished for the student.

Rubrics provide valuable feedback as to what was covered well and what needs further attention. For teachers, rubrics can establish the "needs" for the next time the unit is taught.

Rubrics are accurate measures of objectives.

Rubrics are personalized snapshots of present goals, areas for improvement, current successes and future goals. All of this is accomplished with little or no direct intervention by the teacher since the look-fors and rubric scale paint an accurate picture.

Rubrics establish, before the teaching begins, the focus of the teaching. Both students and teacher begin on the same page with no hidden agenda.

Rubrics allow students the opportunity to determine their own success.

Rubric construction can be taught to students to use for their own personal use. For example, a student could easily rate the amount of effort put into a project as excellent, good, fair or poor based on their own definitions of these terms. The important thing is the student took time to reflect on the effort.

Rubrics are usually done with a scoring form using from 2 to 5 points on the scale. More than that makes differentiating them very difficult. Ideally a rubric scale should have an even number of scale points so the assessor can not take the easy way out and judge a piece of work as in the middle such as could happen on a 3 or 5 point scale.

Scale numbers can easily be converted to letter grades or percentages if necessary.

Rubrics are used to rate performances and are especially important for work that is difficult to measure objectively. By specifying the "indicators" prior to the work being assessed it makes assessment and evaluation much easier. Holistic assessment is difficult when it comes to recommendations for improvement. Rubrics help here!

Rubrics allow assessment to be more objective and consistent from assignment to assignment. Students know exactly what is expected of her/him.

Rubrics provide focus for the teacher to clarify what he/she is going to teach and emphasize this time ignoring other criteria not yet taught or taught previously but not a focus of attention right now. There is nothing wrong with including criteria which have been previously taught and in fact it is encouraged, but the students need to be made aware of that. Giving students the rubric before teaching the lesson or unit of study is a good step. It gives them a focus for learning.

Rubrics also provide the teacher with an opportunity to reflect on the success or lack of success in his/her teaching performance. If the results of the rubric assessment indicate a weakness by the students in general, the focus should be on one or the other of teaching method used and/or the need for more work.

Rubrics measure progress. Giving the same or similar assignments over a period of time allows the teacher to reflect on the rubric results and measure progress. Taking the time to share the progress with individual students, the class, colleagues… is important. Too often we focus on what hasn't been accomplished rather than what has been accomplished. Celebrate successes!

Rubrics are designed to measure a clearly stated objective. There is a specific target to be measured. The rating system provides a range of possibilities rather than an all or none approach. The criteria for each of the ratings are measures of different degrees of success according to what has been taught.

Rubrics are dynamic. They are not static. As the students progress and the teacher progresses, the rubrics change to reflect that growth. Rubrics can be easily made class specific or even student specific.

Rubrics designed for self-assessment can be used by the teacher to form a part of the student's final evaluation and/or for diagnostic purposes to help set goals for individual students and/or the entire class.

## RUBRIC TERMINOLOGY

### Scale Length

The above scale has a length of 4. Scale length is the number of choices you have on the scale. An even number of scale points eliminates the ability of the assessor to simply take the middle ground depending on the descriptors. You can have a scale length of 2 or more. Bear in mind that the more choice you have the more difficult it will be to differentiate between the choices.

### Scale Points

In the above scale the scale points are the numbers 1 - 2- 3- 4. This could also be D,C,B,A or Poor, Fair, Very Good, Excellent or 55%, 65%, 75%,85% or any other names you want to give them.

### Descriptors

The descriptors are the look-fors, criteria, qualifiers, objectives, checklist items, targets… that should be demonstrated in the work in order to receive that rating on the scale.

For example, to create a rubric assessment for a descriptive paragraph written by a student for self-evaluation, peer evaluation or teacher evaluation I might suggest the following. I am using a very simple example here of three different criteria only but you could add as many as you taught in the lesson leading up to the assignment. Students should know what they are expected to do before they are asked to do it and know exactly how they will be assessed.

For this example I shall use only three criteria—number of sentences, proper use of adjectives and adverbs and a good closing/summary sentence. These criteria were taught during the lessons.

## Level 1

a minimum of 6 sentences
a minimum of 6 adjectives and/or adverbs correctly used
a poor closing/summary sentence

## Level 2

minimum 7–8 sentences
minimum 7–8 adjectives/adverbs correctly used
a fair closing sentence

## Level 3

minimum 9–10 sentences
minimum 9–10 adjectives/adverbs correctly used
a good closing sentence

## Level 4

11 or more sentences
11 or more adjectives/adverbs correctly used
an excellent closing sentence

**Note:** Each of these levels which are currently numbers 1–4 can be easily converted to letter grades or percentages or descriptors if needed. But in most cases for assessments you need not do that until you get to the evaluation stage.

You may have to use some judgment to decide between two different levels if most of the criteria are met but not all of them. In those situations you can assign the lower of the two levels which would be justifiable or you can return the work to the student to make the necessary changes to move him/her up a level. By exercising this option you are teaching the student what she/he needs to do to move ahead. Your objective is to get the most out of every teaching situation to help the student establish a new "base level" of work. Rubrics can be powerful motivators.

## RUBRIC DESIGN SUGGESTIONS

**Note:**   an Internet search will yield plenty of examples of rubrics.

**A note of caution:** too often rubrics are too complicated and require too much time to do the assessment. Keep everything as simple as possible.

Make a list of the concepts, skills or standards you are assessing. Create a rubric for each one if necessary along with descriptors. From the list you can then edit it to a manageable number. Don't overdo it. Simplify the list so time spent doing the assessment is reasonable under the circumstances.

In creating a rubric, it is important that you can easily identify what it is you are measuring for each of the rubrics. You do not want to spend more time than necessary to circle the scale point that best describes the work done.

Determine the number of scale points that best suits the assessment. That could be as few as two or as many as 8 or 10 but remember that the more scale points you have the more difficult it will be to differentiate and the more time you will have to spend in the analysis. Aim for 2 to 6 with no even numbers unless it fits the situation. Four points is probably the most common number.

Next list the descriptors that will differentiate the numbers of names of the scale. For example, if the scale is excellent, good, fair, poor then you would describe what the project or assignment would need to include for it to be rated excellent as well as each of the other scale point labels. You would then list them.

Another option for creating a rubric scale is to make a list of the 10 look-fors you have for the project or assignment then determine the scale using the number of

these look-fors that are found in the project. For example, you may get an A if you have 9 or 10 of the look-fors in your project; a B for 7–8 look-fors present; a C for 5–6 look-fors present and a D for 4 or fewer. This check-list approach works well for the students who need to know what they need to do to get an A or any other grade they feel they can attain.

Use the rubric for self-evaluation, peer evaluation or teacher evaluation comparing the performance to the rubric scale and descriptors. Record the scale achieved for each student. You can easily convert any rubric scale into a letter grade or percentage mark if you use the 4 point scale if that is what you are mandated to do for report cards.

Take a few minutes to reflect on the rubric in terms of its effectiveness so you can make any necessary changes to improve the rubric and measure what you want to measure. Don't hesitate to ask students for their input on the effectiveness of your rubric. Rubrics are dynamic. Does this rubric measure what it is intended to measure? Does this rubric need more or fewer scale points to accurately measure what you want to measure? Is there enough differentiation among the scale point descriptors?

## SOME FINAL THOUGHTS

1. It is very possible to design rubrics with only 2 scale points. This is a yes-no or pass-fail mentality but it can be a quick way for the teacher and student to make an effective assessment.

Some possibilities for scale point labels are: yes-no; pass-no pass; pass-redo; acceptable-unacceptable; accomplished-not accomplished; demonstrated-not demonstrated; done-not done…

2. Three point rubrics are effective in some situations. Bear in mind that having an odd number of points on the scale allows the assessor to choose the middle ground unless the descriptors are very specific. For example, a rubric of good-fair-poor without descriptors would find many assessors choosing fair without looking carefully at the descriptors. But good descriptors will force the assessor to choose the best one among the three choices. The list of descriptors should be clearly differentiated among each of the scale points.

3. Descriptors or look-fors for each point can be created using adjectives or adverbs. For example, in assessing whether or not the student had good summary sentences for each paragraph you may include words like always, most of the time, some of the time or very few times. You could include the number of paragraphs where the summary sentence was a good one if the total number of paragraphs was assigned.

4. By creating a list of look-fors as a check-list for assessment you can then quickly check them off for each student's

work. By giving letter grades based on the total number of items on the check-list that were done according to expectations, you can convert that check-list number into a letter grade as mentioned above. This is a very effective way to do assessments of projects.

**Note**: for project work don't wait for the project to be completed before beginning the assessment. You can save marking time and give direction to students before they go astray and ruin the entire project. You also have at least some marks should the student not turn in the final project or "the dog ate it".

5. Once you have established the rubrics they can be used over and over again. You will soon have a collection of rubrics upon which to draw and you can adapt to various situations.

6. If you have several rubrics for a subject or project and you require a final mark or grade you can "weight" them so your final evaluation reflects the full body of work that has been assessed. This is where your judgment as a teacher enters the picture. You will have several assessments upon which to base your final evaluation and to justify it if necessary. Keep a record of the reasons for your weighted judgments.

For example, you may have a major project or examination as the main focus but other work can move the final evaluation up or down depending on the quality of work done.

7. The best rubrics are the ones that the teacher creates to meet her/his needs. Creating your own rubrics also makes the assessment go much quicker and smoother because you created them. There is no confusion about what it is that you want to measurer and what you are looking for. Using someone else's rubrics can make more work for you.

**Design your own rubrics to meet your needs and the needs of the students.**

The more you do it, the easier it becomes and the more effective they will be.

8. Rubric scales must be created before you teach not after you have finished the unit of study for example. It is perfectly okay to make changes as you go along but keep the students informed of any changes in terms of what is to be assessed and how it is to be assessed.

9. Rubric creation will become second nature to you and your students the more you use them. Rubrics will save you time and effort. Final evaluations will be much easier to do and you will be better prepared to support your final evaluation with data not just your professional opinion.

Think Rubric! Think Assessment and Evaluation!

# STUDENT MOTIVATION

## Effective Methods For Motivating Students

*Marjan Glavac*

By now you've learned that there is no one thing that works in education. It is a combination of best practices used consistently that produces results.

Students want a teacher that knows them personally and cares about them as an individual, has a sense of humor, is organized and on time, knows what they're talking about, hands back assignments in a reasonable time, makes lessons interesting, uses technology, has fun.

Here's an earlier quote that's worth repeating:

**According to a Toronto Star newspaper survey on Education, this is how students described the ideal teacher—**

*"… the ideal teacher is a person who actually teaches, who acts like a human being, and who tries to look attractive."*

The biggest motivator in the class is you. You are the most important factor of success for students. To enable students who may never have experienced success to experience it, you must show them. You must have that bag of tricks, those tools to motivate them when they are failing, when they get off track, when they want to give up. When all is said and done, you cannot control students. The only person you can control is yourself and your reaction to an event. In this session, I'm going to discuss the best practices that work to motivate students and prevent misbehavior before it happens.

## # 1 You Are The Key

Since **YOU** are **THE MOST IMPORTANT FACTOR IN THE CLASSROOM**, let's start with you.

Take care of yourself physically, emotionally and spiritually. As the well used quote says "If your buckets aren't full, how can you fill up student's buckets?" Fill up your buckets by giving yourself permission to do things for yourself. Right now I'm giving you permission to take care of yourself. Set aside time for yourself every day to do something you like to do. This time may be in the morning before everyone gets up, during your lunch hour, after school when all the kids have left, or just before bedtime when everyone has turned in for the night. No one is going to take care of you as well as you can. No one knows you as well as you do. Go for a walk, visit the health club and work out, go for a swim, read something pleasurable, practice a hobby, meditate, visit a friend, listen to music, watch a movie.

Some techniques I use for stress reduction include: a sponge ball in the shape of an apple that I squeeze as many times as there are days left in the school year. This parent present really calms me down; Writing down all the negative things that happened that day on a piece of paper and crumpling it up and throwing it away in the trash bin; phoning one of your good students and telling the parent how much you appreciate their child; stopping by a park by the river on the way home from school to unwind from a stressful day. I spend a few moments to admire the river, the rowers, the kayakers, the birds, the bicyclists and joggers, and let all the cares of the day melt away before I go home. I also take time to meditate, go to the gym, to run, swim, do weights and visit the sauna and steam room as often as I can!

Eat something nutritious for those low energy times in the day. A piece of fruit, an energy bar, yogurt will tie you over. Keep up your energy by doing daily physical activities with your students. If you don't have time to work out in a health club, this is a great alternative. Students will see you in a positive light and burn off some of their energy at the same time. Some of the activities I do with students include walking or running up the stairs, deep knee bends or squats in class. I do these squats with the students when waiting outside other classes they go to such as their music class or technology class. Instead of having them wait outside the class doing nothing, I do these deep knee bends with them. This activity not only settles them done, but it gives me an opportunity to squeeze in some daily physical activity for them and for myself.

The latest research on teacher burnout shows that teachers who are least likely to burn out are those who discuss positive aspects of the job with other teachers and associate pleasant emotions with the job. Negative thoughts are energy vampires.

This takes us back to the exercise we did on goal setting and finding your interests, values, and passions. Tie your teaching to your interests, values and passions. Students will respond much more positively to a teacher who shows enthusiasm for a subject than one who complains about it. If you're broadcasting the message that you're not interested or are bored with your teaching and subject matter, students will mirror this back to you. Students take your "temperature" every minute of the day. They're checking you out looking for your "buttons".

To achieve success in the classroom, you need to know yourself. You need to feel right in your own skin. To enable students who may never have experienced success to experience it, you must show them. If students who may never have experienced success are going to experience success, they must see success in you. You must exude success; be a model of success to them.

Knowing yourself means taking a hard, close, and objective look at who you are. This can be a painful process, but it need not be if you're honest with yourself. To come face to face with your own weaknesses, limitations, fears, and doubts isn't easy. However, if you don't do it, your students will. They will find out your triggers, your buttons, your stress points. You must find them first.  Your strengths, your hopes, dreams and goals, are the sparks that light the fire of desire in you to teach. They keep you going in those dark depressing days when nothing seems to go right- those days when you feel like giving up. Every teacher has them at some point. You must overcome them. Then bounce back determined to succeed. In addition to the goal setting exercise, here are here are some questions that will help you get to know yourself:

What do you personally like/dislike about yourself?

What motivated you to become a teacher?

What are your hobbies, interests and talents?

What do you like/dislike about children?

What do you like to do when you are free to do what you want to do?

What are your most memorable moments? What made them so?

Give an example how different people may have found it memorable for different reasons. E.g. a birthday: I was the center of attention; I planned it; It was great-everyone had a great time; I got my first motorbike etc.

Here's an approach I've found that helped me discover my interests and talents. In high school I took a general interest inventory. It showed I had a high interest in writing, perhaps because I loved to read so much. At the end of my university studies I took the *Strong-Campbell Interest Inventory* now know as the *Strong Interest Inventory* (SII) This is a vocational interest assessment tool. (My daughter has also taken it recently before deciding on her university courses.) Not surprisingly, English teacher was in the top 3, right below lawyer and reporter. I also learned which subjects and careers least interested me. At the time I didn't give the revelations much thought. However, after teaching a number of years, those weaknesses show up in the classroom.

Interest inventories can confirm what you may already suspect! Knowing what I'm weak in has helped me a great deal. By taking additional courses, asking colleagues for help and advice and even asking my own students for ideas, I've strengthened my skills. Discovering your weaknesses yourself is a lot easier than finding them out from your students or during a job evaluation.

Now you have come face to face with your strengths and weaknesses. Now you know your limitations and expectations. Once you become comfortable with who you are and you truly know yourself, playing to your strengths and the strengths of your students will become easier. It will also be easier to offset or improve, and to help your students to do the same. Only when you can accept "you", will you be able to accept your students.

I found it easier to admit to my students that I can't sing, dance, draw, or do a lot of other things, than fake that I can or to tell them otherwise. Finally admitting to yourself and to others your weaknesses, especially if you are a closet perfectionist, is actually liberating! In doing so, you will better appreciate your students' strengths and weaknesses.

Start now to go into your class with the attitude that every day you will learn something from your students and they will learn something from you. Be yourself in front of them. Resolve to do your best every day. In doing so, you will be taking the first steps toward making a real difference in your classroom. As you do your best, you will inspire your students to do their best.

## Quench the Flames of Burnout

Here are some things you can do to deal with burnout and stress: (Just be sure more work doesn't add to more stress.)

- Take on a new task such as a school or district committee.

- Enroll in a fun workshop, seminar or conference or personal, non-teaching interest.

- Change teaching grade assignments in the school.

- Change schools.

- Go into a different teaching role such as resource, administration.

- Avoid the negative attitude of your colleagues. Be more positive.

- Cultivate a hobby.

- Take a leave of absence.

- Eat healthier.

- Get exercise.

- Enroll in a yoga, Pilates, Tai Chi, aerobic course.

- Take up swimming, jogging, walking, rowing, cycling.

- Get a physical checkup.

- Get enough sleep.

- Use deep breathing, meditation techniques, music to relax.

- Attitude is a choice, choose your attitude.

- Pick your battles: your hill to "die" on.

- Keep things in perspective.

- Have realistic, attainable, and measurable goals.

- Cultivate allies among students, staff, and parents.

- Find friends outside of teaching.

- Go to out-of-town conferences.

- Give Pat On The Backs, and send thank-you notes, cards, and compliments to others. Why not send one to yourself.

- Send yourself some flowers.

- Develop positive self-talk, self-control, and self-confidence.

- Cultivate a sense of humor; laugh and smile more.

- Join a professional reading group.

- Participate in a noon hour walking club.

- Give yourself a gift of time to reflect, relax, and recharge.

- Define what success is for you, not for others.

- Believe in yourself.

- Practice random acts of kindness.

- Read motivational quotes, and stories.

- Collect and mount motivational posters in your classroom.

- Take a vacation, a week-end getaway, or go to a spa retreat.

- Find a significant other who can support you in good times and bad.

- Get involved with your professional teacher groups.

- Learn how to say no—you don't have to do it all.

- Replace the words can't, try, and problems with can, will, and challenges.

- Be flexible, or you'll be permanently bent out of shape.

- Focus on the positive.

- Join a sports league or a charitable volunteer group.

- Get a pet (rabbit, cat, dog…).

- Do your best. Perfection is the enemy of excellence. There is a very wide range of good, acceptable, yet valuable work. "Perfect" teachers are a burden to everyone-even themselves.

## #2 Rapport between teacher and students

Get to know your students. Before school begins, start watching TV shows and movies that your students would watch. Listen to their music and radio stations. Visit some of their favorite websites. Play their video games. Find out how an iPod works. Listen to the language they use and try to understand what it means! If you have elementary or high school students, they will quickly correct you on what the "new lingo" means. The words "cool" and "hot" mean the same thing!

Take the time to review their student files and portfolios before school begins. Once the information is collected, review it with the help of a specialist teacher or a Learning Resource Teacher. Students with apparent difficulties can be flagged for extra help and resources depending on the personnel and resources available in the school. On the first day of school and during that first week, I will gather additional information on my students in other ways. For example, I will test students' spelling ability using the Morrison McCall Spelling Scale. Then I will do this once a term using the initial test as a baseline.

To assess reading skill level, I administer the McCall Crabbs Standard Test Lessons In Reading. I do three tests timed for three minutes the first day and then another three the next day. Doing so gives me a baseline of their reading and provides me some information for their reading groups. At the end of the year, I retest the first three tests. I also use the Developmental Reading Assessment or DRA to evaluate reading about 6–7 weeks into the first term. I also add my own grade level reading passages and do a running record with them every 6 weeks. This way I can get a good handle on where my students are and what I need to teach them to get them to the grade level standards. In Math, I do a quick review of numeracy (adding, subtracting, multiplying, dividing) using questions of increasing difficulty. Again, I retest at the end of the year to measure progress. I also give out a number of different surveys to learn more about students' extracurricular interests and learning styles.

## #3 Best Sources Of Information – And How To Get Them

One of my best sources of information are the informal conversations I have with other teachers. They often prove invaluable, especially when a student exhibits extraordinary or unusual behavior. A simple mention of the behavior to a teacher who has taught the student and/or a sibling the previous year may be all I need to uncover the underlying cause of the student's behavior.

Perhaps one of the most valuable sources of information on students is their parents. Early in the school year, most schools have a parent—teacher open house night. It is sometimes known as "Meet the Creature". I make calls to parents reminding them about the event. I also say something positive about each child and then ask if the parent has any questions or concerns about the first days of school. I also ask if there is anything they would like me to know about their child. Often what they say comes as a surprise to me, so I thank them for sharing that information.

Another technique used by my colleagues, is to ask for a letter written by the parent on the strengths and weaknesses of their child.

During the open house, parents again will share with me information that may not be written down. Parents tell me about a child's summer, winning a competition, or wanting to do a certain thing in my class during the year.

All this information gives me a valuable understanding of who my students are, of the challenges I have, the way I need to teach, and the resources both physical and human I may need to meet those challenges. Keep accurate quotes, take notes of what parents say. Make appropriate observation notes.

Once you've gotten to know your students, you can zero in and focus on the class as a whole and on individual students that might present future hotspots.

## The Scavenger Hunt

First, let's deal with the class as a whole.

On that very first day of school, I use a number of exercises to promote class bonding. One activity which I suggest as a way to get to know your students, is a student scavenger hunt. This sheet lists challenges and tasks such as "Find someone who is: new to our school; has visited 3 countries; is left handed; is the oldest in their family; has seen two oceans, and so forth. There are 3 reasons I like to do this on the very first day of school:

It gives me the opportunity the very first day to observe interactions among students. I learn about the personalities of students. Here, I see who are the natural leaders and or followers, students who have high self-esteem and those who lack confidence, students who tend to be loud and boisterous, and others who are shy and quiet, students who have many friends, students who have very few friends. This activity also pinpoints students who are needy by the number of times they come up to ask me for the answers to the questions on their sheet.

The scavenger hunt is the perfect opportunity to start to take pictures and to videotape students for my own video time capsule of their progress. I usually videotape 2-5 minutes of certain highlights several times during the school year. Doing so usually gives me between 45-60 minutes of video which I show to students on the very last day of school.

The activity is also a way of making every student in your class special. It is a non-threatening activity. There are no right or wrong answers. There are no marks to earn. If an answer can't be found, I let students leave the space blank. The answers are taken up as a class, discussed and collected. They are not evaluated and students are told this. Since the assignment is done in class, every student is able to do it. Consequently, their first assignment is complete. They've achieved success on their very first assignment.

The group scavenger hunt contains such topics as their birth order, whether they are left or right handed, whether they are born outside the country. I try to do this in a non-threatening manner by having a short class discussion after the completion of the survey on what it means to be the only child in the family, the youngest child, the middle child, the oldest child, or a child in a large family. We also talk about the challenges of being left handed. To find out about students who were born outside the country, we have interesting discussions on different cultures, languages and religions. Doing this gives me the opportunity to show the class how diverse a group we are. We are all different, yet we are all in the same class together.

## #4 Student Needs

Students come into your class with a number of concerns and questions. High achieving students want to know how they will be graded and what they need to do to get excellent marks. Low achieving, high needs, and special education students want to know what kind of person the teacher is. They want to know whether the teacher is going to like them or not.

I focus on students with high needs as early as possible in the school year. Then, I have a better chance of reaching them and changing their behavior. I have few, if any negative perceptions of them. Moreover, I have the greatest amount of energy at the beginning of the year than I do at any other time!

If I'm teaching in a school where I've taught for a year or more, I have a good idea who these students are from my dealings with them on the playground, and in the hallways, assemblies, and through conversations with other teachers. Certain students keep coming up more often than others. Another advantage is that I get to know their names very quickly! Hopefully, I've been able to find something positive about each student, especially if I know he or she are coming into my class the next year. I may have even taught their brother or sister and therefore might be able to form a connection based on that relationship. Often I notice a strength in them while they were on the playground during sports or extracurricular activities. Whatever it may be, I try hard to build at least one connection before students come to my class.

One of the first things I do, and what I've found to be extremely effective, is to catch those students doing something positive the very first day. And since I've usually made that very first day a very busy yet non-threatening day, finding something positive is not hard. And when I find that positive "something" I make a "sunshine call" to their parents. This is a phone call to give parents positive news. It is very effective first because parents of students who are often in trouble at school don't get usually get these calls, and second because we tend to phone parents to give them bad news rather than good news.

Sunshine calls are a great way of building rapport early in the year with parents and with your high needs students. Building rapport early encourages students to work with you even when things aren't going well. Moreover, you likely will get much needed support from parents when you need it. If you can get a parent on your side early, behavior problems are easier to solve.

Every new lesson, new goal, new learning experience can be an exciting time for you. It can be an anxious time for students. Every new situation is a change for students. This can cause anxiety. Some students thrive on the new challenges, some hide with worry and fear. Find out what worries your students and makes them anxious. Show them how to overcome their anxiety. Demonstrate empathy, and understanding about their worries. This approach will give them help, hope, and inspiration. It will help them move out of their present position of anxiety into a more comfortable one. Once students are more comfortable with you and your lessons, they will become more accepting of the challenges and goals you have for them.

One way to minimize stress in your assignments is to arrange students to do them in partners or in groups. Before students do the assignment, have them get to know each other. I ask them to ask each other what they're doing on the weekend, or a question on a personal hobby or interest the class may not know about. Change partners and groups often. I do this randomly by picking names out of a container on my desk. In this way, you not only lessen stress in assignments, you also build up class bonds. The more students know about each other, the safer they will feel.

An effective activity for this is the use of a community circle time. Students get to leave their desks to sit in a regularly scheduled community circle on the carpet. I usually schedule this as a first thing on Monday mornings and the last thing on Friday afternoons. Sometimes I will bring in a treat which is shared among all the students. Each student voluntarily shares what he or she did on the weekend or will be doing on the weekend. Sometimes the community circle time is used during the week as a way to discuss certain topics. I have also used it to recognize students who have achieved a goal or contributed to the class or school in a positive way.

I find the community circle time to be a great opportunity to build class rapport and teamwork skills.

Students who have a sense of belonging, do better socially and academically. They experience less conflict with their peers and their teachers. They are also more trusting and more willing to take on new challenges in a supportive classroom.

Ask students to use a "thumbs up" sign if they understand the concepts that you are teaching or a "thumbs down" sign if they don't understand. Have them silently mouth the answers to you. This works well for one word answers, or Math problems.

Allow students to have choices. You may want students to have input into your rules, procedures, working in partners or groups, classroom setup, seating arrangement, classroom duties. The more choices students have will give them a feeling of more control and ownership of what happens in the classroom.

## Some Final Suggestions...

Give feedback often. Focus on your students' growth and not on their intelligence or abilities. Show them how they're growing by comparing what they first did in your class and what they're doing now. Give them feedback when they fail by showing them what went wrong with their strategy and how they can do it better.

Create an interesting learning environment by building up credibility in your lessons by making them real. Connect them to your students' interests, abilities and to their world for maximum impact. One way to do this is to go back to the interest surveys you did at the beginning of the year. Another way is to greet them at the door and ask them about their weekend, their goals, their interest. Keep lessons short. Give specific directions. Show examples of what is expected. Anticipate your students' questions and fears about lessons and subjects by easing their fears of new material. Do this by giving students strategies that worked for you, that worked for other students.

Let students get to know you too. Set up a spot in your class displaying your articles, awards, and photos of you outside of school. If you play a musical instrument, bring it in. If you have a pet, show the students. I still remember my grade 2 teacher bringing in her iguana pet to show us. We had never seen an iguana before. Another teacher brought in a lobster shell from a meal she had the night before. Again, none of us had ever seen a lobster shell before. Bring in your pictures of your travels. All this sharing will let students get to know as a real person and not just as a teacher. Let them know why you became a teacher. Show them your enthusiasm for your subject. Share with them how you overcome obstacles in school to get where you are now. Be yourself. Don't try and be someone that you aren't.

Variety is the spice of life. By using a variety of teaching methods, you'll prevent boredom, maintain student interest and involvement. Bring in guest speakers, recruit volunteers, bring in a fellow teacher to teach your class, celebrate birthdays, participate in round table discussions, role playing, simulations, games, field trips, special theme days, class parties. In short, have fun!

# APPENDIX

## Handout

## Know Your Students Student Review Sheet

| | | | |
|---|---|---|---|
| Name of Parent/ Guardian | | Testing Results | Reading ______ <br> Writing ______ <br> Math ______ |
| Custody | | Academic Assessments (Gifted) | |
| Date of Birth | ___ ___ ___ | Violent Incident Reports | |
| Age as of: | | Suspension Letters | |
| Retained | Yes/No Grade(s) ____ | Psychological Report | |
| Number of Schools Since Kindergarten | | Speech and Language Report | |
| Absent/Lates last year | Ab = ______ <br> Lates = ______ | Learning and Behavior Report | |
| Social/Emotional Concerns | | Information re: Medication | |
| Physical Concerns | | Occupational Therapy | |
| Language Concerns | | Hearing Acuity | |
| Math Concerns | | Last IEP Review Date | |
| IEP Exceptionalilty | | Initial IEP Date | |
| Present Address: Present Phone # | | Other Notes | |

# Behavior Management–Data to the Rescue

*Paul Jackson*

*The Data Collection Method of Behavior Management*

## Behavior cards

Experience gained after 30 years as both a classroom teacher and a school administrator led me to the conclusion that the ability to manage behavior of students (and teachers) was through data collection.

It is no longer, nor has it ever been, acceptable to denounce someone's behavior without evidence of what has happened and what has been done to correct the behavior. That evidence is the data collected and recorded in a logical fashion.

It is also imperative that a "team" of people is involved with any kind of behavior management program. That team must all be convinced that there is a problem; in other words acknowledge the problem, before any change can take place. Most of all the person whose behavior needs changed must be painfully made aware of what the problem is, how and who it affects, and acknowledge that there is a problem. This is a Dr. Philism!

"You can not change what you do not acknowledge."—Dr. Phil

Then and only then can change take place. It is the data that convinces the individual there is a problem and the data that convinces the people who are affected by the problem to help do something about it.

It is the data collected after some form of intervention that also measures the success of the team in changing behavior.

Your job, as a team member, is not to make the changes needed by the individual but to set up a system whereby the individual changes him/herself but not without some outside intervention and support.

As a classroom teacher or school administrator you may be the key person to initiate some form of behavior modification but you are not a "one man/woman team".

The intention of this report is to convince you of the importance of collecting data in order to modify behavior. It is not a report on how to modify the behavior. Your team can do that. But if you are to be the catalyst for change, you must begin with the fundamental belief that raw, objective data is the starting point.

## The "Behavior card" system explained

The foundation of data collection for behavior modification is the "Behavior Card" system. I have used this method both in the classroom and for an entire school (for students). I have taught classroom teachers to use this same system which is easy to set up, easy to maintain and extremely successful at changing behavior.

The "cards" referred to are index cards that you can purchase at any office supply company. You probably have hundreds sitting around in your school or home right now. The size doesn't matter but I recommend larger rather than smaller so they don't become lost and you have plenty of room on a single card for data.

You may want to have a secure place to store the cards as the information on them is personal and shouldn't be accessible to anyone other than someone who has been given permission to use them. Legally they are your personal notes and not community property. But bear in mind that under some circumstances the police may subpoena your notes or your school board may do so. You must be careful to record only substantiated objective data on your cards. Never record your opinions or judgments.

**Note:** It is not recommended that you use a computer driven system because it removes one of the great benefits of the card system— the ability to select a card(s) of a student(s) and share the contents regardless of where you might be. It is beneficial that students see and "feel" the card when the time comes. Portability is important. It is also less time consuming because you record your notes only once and immediately when the occurrence happens. You do not have to then transfer the information to the computer.

It is convenient that you have a box in which to store the cards. Arrange the cards in some logical fashion. The most common would be alphabetically by last name but different situations may make some other way better. For example, I often arranged students by their home room classroom teacher then alphabetically.

Create a card when the need arises. Don't make cards up for all your students. That isn't necessary and maybe sends a message that at one time or another all students will have a card. You will be surprised at how few cards you may have in a classroom or a school.

Keep the record-keeping simple. The basic information is name, date, problem and consequences. Options are: parents' names, teacher's name, home phone number, extenuating circumstances… but these can be added under the consequences if needed or attached to the card or put on the back of the card for easy reference when making contact.

Write legibly so students can read the comments. That may mean printing them for the younger students.

## Name

Record the student's full name at the top of the card and highlight it so you can easily find it.

## Date

On the left hand side of the card, record the date of the occurrence including the date(s) when you talked to the student.

## Problem—Description

Next to the date briefly describe the problem. Include all relevant information for easy future reference. Leave space to the right of this column for the consequences. If other students were involved with the student note that. If witnesses were involved record that. Record the teacher making the report unless that was you. Be specific **after** gathering all the information. These notes are a summary of what you have learned. These notes will help you remember the incident at a future meeting with the student, parents, teacher, police, outside agency… You will learn quickly just how much or how little to record.

**Note:**  You can always use these notes to write a full report if necessary.

**Note:**  It is a good idea to have the Problem column and Consequences column side by side for easier reference.

## Consequences

This last column is for the consequences of the problem behavior. In some situations there may not be any consequences except for the recording the incident on the card.

**Note:**  I refer to this as having "carded" the individual with no other consequences. You will find students referring to "being carded" by the teacher or principal "Carding" becomes a consequence in and of itself. The simple fact that a student's behavior is "permanently recorded" for future use in case the problem re-occurs is disturbing to students. It's like having a criminal record but as you will see later under the guidelines for using Behavior Cards, it is not a permanent record for most students.

The consequences may be whatever you deem appropriate at the time. As stated earlier just recording the incident may be all that is done. You may have give a detention, have the student write a letter of apology, write a letter to his/her parents explaining what happened, write out the rule(s) broken, make a promise or declaration to change his/her behavior, classroom or school suspension, ask the student to state the rule, do community service, do extra work around the school, a warning of future consequences, a meeting with teachers, a meeting with parents or guardians, removal of privileges, loss of yard or recess time, withdrawal of excursion privileges… You get the idea.

There must **always** be consequences. They must all be recorded. Do not rely on your memory as to what was done. The consequences tell you what was tried, what worked and what didn't work. Consequences will naturally escalate depending on the behavior pattern.

Time gaps of short duration or long duration between similar behaviors would warrant different consequences. Different kinds of behavior may require different consequences. Isolated problems aren't likely to be treated as seriously as ones that indicate a pattern.

**Patty Nasjack**

**Grade 6; Mrs. Curlytoes**

| Date | Description | Consequences |
| --- | --- | --- |
| Oct 9 | Bullying Samantha Hopeful (same classroom) on School yard at recess; warned; Repeated it; Mr. Pills; several witnesses confirmed; problem about name calling | warning about bullying; reminder about school policy; loss of yard privileges Oct 10–12 warning further bullying will mean parents called Apology to Samantha |

# How Can You Make Good Use of these Behavior Cards?

### Counselling One-on-One

Use the information on the cards in counselling sessions with the student. It is sometimes a good idea to give the cards to the student to read for her/himself to reinforce why this counselling session is needed. Make sure to record your counselling session date, what was discussed and the action plan (consequence) that was agreed upon. Keep these notes up to date.

Discuss with the student any patterns you are seeing. Take note of the dates of the recorded data to indicate times when the behavior was improving.

### Conferences

Use these notes for parent conferences or meetings with support staff, Principal, other teachers, outside agencies… where the student's behavior is being discussed.

One strategy that works well is to mail a copy of the Behavior Cards to the parents before the conference along with an explanation of the card system itself. In this way you make better use of your conference time. You also give the parents an opportunity to talk to their child before the meeting.

I also suggest that the student be present for all or some of every conference. He/she needs to know exactly what everyone has agreed to and deserves to have input into the consequences of the meeting. Too often the "agenda" of the parents affects the message taken home to the student. Avoid any confusion by having all the stake-holders present to hear everything and provide their input.

## Patterns of Behavior

Keeping accurate records will allow you to look for patterns of behavior that may otherwise have gone unnoticed. For example, that student's worst problems are with one teacher not all the teachers; the problems occur most frequently on Mondays which may be weekends he/she spends with the non-custodial parent; that the student gets into trouble with a certain group she/he hangs around with; that there are one or two individual students who are the targets…

The frequency of the problems may warrant more attention than the seriousness of the problems. The time gap between the problems may mean the student is seriously working at getting better or isn't doing a thing to make things better. The problems may be escalating in intensity. Certain consequences may be having better results than others. Parental involvement may be key to the changed behavior.

## Consequences

When you record the consequences you have tried you will be better able to decide what is working and what isn't. It is perfectly okay to reward good behavior with a positive consequence and record that as well. You will also have a list of everything you have tried in your "bag of tricks".

## Setting Goals

The behavior cards can be used very effectively to set goals for the student. By focussing on the problem areas you can devise action plans that will help the student solve his/her problems and find ways to cope with situations that are causing her/him problems.

## Requests for Help

Teachers can use the information on Behavior Cards to help make their case when they are requesting additional support from the Principal, support from inside the school system, agencies outside the school system or any individual or group that would strengthen the team to help modify serious behavior problems.

## Positive Progress Reports

Periodically a teacher or Principal who uses these Behavior Cards can talk to a student who isn't currently in trouble and talk in a positive manner about the improvements noted. The principle that you should try to catch someone doing something right is applied to the cards as well. When you note a student doing something that in the past he/she would have done inappropriately, it is time to bring out the cards and discuss the progress. Make note of this meeting as well.

Of course you will use the cards to denote any lack of progress as well.

## Report Cards

Having the Behavior Cards at your disposal makes doing the report cards much easier. You have plenty of data to back up your professional judgment when it comes to social skills and general behavior patterns. You can write your report with confidence and will have good information to share with parents during the follow-up conference.

# Some General Points
# About the Behavior Card System

## 1. Every Time

Every time an inappropriate behavior happens that is serious enough to warrant an intervention, then some form of intervention should occur. This intervention may take the form of a gesture, a look, a checkmark, a stare, a rule reminder, a note on the behavior card (we will get to this soon), a token given out… If the behavior warrants it, record it on the card and tell the student you have done it.

## 2. Keep It Simple and Accurate

Keep your data notes short and to the point. Discuss the problem with the student and any witnesses before making your final recording to accurately capture the final outcome of the "investigation".

## 3. Be Expedient and Thorough

Deal with each and every problem as quickly as possible without wasting everyone's time but still doing what is necessary. Knowing you have the card data to rely on, you don't have to spend a lot of time rehashing the "old stuff" you just have to acknowledge it.

## 4. Data is More Powerful than Opinion

It is one thing to say a student's behavior is "bad" or "inappropriate", it's quite another to say, "Johnny has interrupted the classroom on an average of 8 times a day for the last two weeks to the point where I had to stop teaching." That is the power of data that you have collected over the two week span.

Data is powerful. Students respect that data more than they do the teacher's opinion. Data is often irrefutable. Data jumps out at you differently than opinion. Data is powerful!

## 5. You Can Not Change What Is Not Acknowledged

Inappropriate behavior can only be changed if it is acknowledged by the student. Data helps the student realize the nature and extent of the problem. Those most affected by the problem behavior and those who are responsible for helping the student make changes will acknowledge the problem if the data is compelling.

## 6. Classroom Rules

One of the foundations for a well behaved classroom is establishing jointly with the students and the teacher a set of classroom rules. It is against that standard that the student should be measured. The teacher can always make sure that the classroom rules are one she/he can live with and the students can take some ownership for them. Individual students must come to realize that the group made the rules and she/he must behave within those guidelines. Peer pressure can work wonders at times. This applies equally to school rules.

## 7. Behavior Cards Do Not Solve Behavior Problems

The Behavior Cards are not meant to be the solution to behavior problems. Teachers and Principals will need to seek specific information, help, support, strategies… to deal with the specific problems. The Internet is a great source of help. The professional library in the school system and professional magazines/ organizations as well as training sessions can also help. The Behavior Cards are a vehicle for recognizing, recording, tracking and setting goals for change.

## 8. Focus on the Few; Celebrate the Majority

Do a student analysis of all the students in your class to see exactly who your problem students are and exactly what their problems may be. Focus on the needy ones. Celebrate the ones who are well behaved. You will likely find that you are really only dealing with a few students and by working on each one of them individually you will reduce the overall problems as well. Work first on students with whom you are likely to have success. This reduces the overall work load. Manage, rather than try to modify, the behavior of the worst behaviors until you can get to them.

## 9. The Scope of the Focus

Determine whether or not you are going to record in-classroom behavior problems or out-of-classroom (yard, halls, recesses, lunch room, field trips) behaviors. It is probably a good idea to record all the student problems for students who are assigned to you so you can elicit the help of others if necessary. Remember the team approach. Coordinated cooperation regarding data collection is important. Encourage others who have contact with your major behavior problems to "keep you informed". Keeping you informed doesn't mean you are responsible for the student's behavior.

## 10. Data Earns Respect

Behavior data earns the respect of students, parents, administration, fellow teachers, support staff, and outside agencies. The data show your professional side as a classroom teacher. You are more likely to get help if your appeal for help includes data demonstrating the nature and scope of the problem as well as your past intervention strategies.

## 11. Look for Patterns

Look for patterns in the data as mentioned earlier. By identifying patterns you are demonstrating to others that you have taken the time to analyze the data and reflect upon the information in order to best cope with the problem. Patterns may suggest solutions. Members of the team may better see how their intervention can help change the patterns in a positive way.

## 12. Be Open and Honest About the System

All classroom students should have the Behavior Cards system explained to them the first week of school or before you introduce it if starting during the school year. Explain the method, purpose and uses of the Card System. Tailor how you share this information to your particular age group. Calm any fears that the "good" students may have. Use the term "You will be carded." My experience says that students don't like a permanent record of their behavior. Students will recognize the value of the system from their own personal perspective. For a small investment in time by the teacher to explain the system, the results are well worth it. You will have to make a decision as to whether or not you will share it with the parents and how you will go about doing it. Don't make a bigger deal out of it than necessary. Honesty is important.

## 13. The Clean Slate

Having used the card system on a school-wide basis I would explain the system at a school assembly early in the school year or I would visit each and every classroom to explain the system, review any changes, summarize the previous year from the Principal's perspective, set some school-wide goals and answer questions.

The Behavior Cards from the previous year where shown to the student in a pile held together with an elastic. They were told these cards would be destroyed and that everyone started with a clean slate.

The students were also told that all the cards would be destroyed with the exception of a few students whose behavior from last year did not warrant a clean slate. I told the students that those students whose cards would not be destroyed had already had a meeting with me and I had explained to them why their cards were not destroyed. Those students whose cards were not destroyed could earn the right to have their cards destroyed sometime during the current school year if it was warranted.

## 14. Student Conferences

Conferences with students about their behavior were more productive with the Behavior Card data because you could have them physically hold the cards and read them for themselves. This gave them some reflective time.

You can point out the patterns to the students and discuss the "why" of the pattern as well as possible strategies to change the behavior.

You are able to remind the students just how "bad" or "good" their behavior had been over the past year or month or week.

You emphasize how you (the teacher or principal) want to work with the student to change the inappropriate behavior.

Since consequences, dates and descriptions of the inappropriate behavior were on the card it opened the discussion about what had worked and not worked for every consequence; whether there were large time gaps between misbehaviors and whether the "victims" were the same people or different people. The details were worth discussing. The data provided a crucial starting point for the conference with an expectation that some action plan was needed to remedy the situation.

## 15. Data Takes the Guesswork out of Judgment

Behavior Cards remove the "guesswork" as to the details such as when the problem occurred, how often it happened, what intervention strategies had been tried, who was involved in the situations, the frequency of occurrence, interventions by others, behavior outside and inside the classroom, previous conferences and action plans…

Teachers can speak with confidence, clarity and certainty using the data to support their professional judgment.

## Conclusion

The Student Behavior Card System is the foundation for behavior management in the classroom and in the school.

Do not underestimate the power of data to record the past, see the present and plan for the future.

Data collection and analysis is a powerful tool for change.

# Data Collecting Instruments

The absolute best way to collect the data you want for recording student behavior is to design you very own data collecting instruments.

Included in this handout are two examples of data collecting instruments that could be used to record the information.

**"Individual Student Observation"** is one data instrument that collects virtually everything the student does over a specified time period. This one is best used by someone other than the classroom teacher whose primary function is to observe a single student and record everything the student does. This is objective data with the subjective interpretation to come later.

**"Student Observation—Tally Sheet"** is a data collecting instrument that can be done by a classroom teacher at any time. It can be used for several students at the same time or the same student with several behaviors being recorded.

For example, if you were collecting data on Timothy for leaving his seat you would put Timothy's name in the top part of the first rectangle on the left side. Underneath his name would be "leaving seat". You would then record a check mark (√) or a stroke ( ) for each occurrence of leaving his seat. By breaking the data into mornings and afternoons and each day of the week patterns will emerge that may help identify reasons and solutions.

If you are observing several students with different behaviors you would simply place the students' names and "behavior to be observed" in each respective section and record the data.

A classroom teacher can easily train him/herself to do the recording at natural breaks in the day such as recesses, snack breaks, lunch, spare periods or at the end of the day. It isn't difficult to remember a few students and their behavior when you are already familiar with their inappropriate behavior.

Save your analysis and action plan until you have plenty of data and can reasonably predict that what you are seeing is indeed a pattern that requires attention.

Of course, you can continue tracking the behavior after your intervention and see how the intervention is working. The type of intervention, dates when it was implanted, persons involved with the intervention, subsequent changes to the intervention… should all be recorded.

Like any behavior modification technique, make sure that all the stakeholders are kept informed of the progress or lack of progress.

# STUDENT OBSERVATION—TALLY SHEET

| Student's Name<br>Behaviour<br>Being Observed | MON | | TUES | | WED | | THURS | | FRI | | WEEKLY<br>TOTALS |
|---|---|---|---|---|---|---|---|---|---|---|---|
| | A.M. | PM | A.M. | PM | A.M. | PM | A.M. | PM | A.M. | PM | |
| T= | | | | | | | | | | | |
| T= | | | | | | | | | | | |
| T= | | | | | | | | | | | |
| T= | | | | | | | | | | | |
| T= | | | | | | | | | | | |
| T= | | | | | | | | | | | |
| T= | | | | | | | | | | | |
| T= | | | | | | | | | | | |
| T= | | | | | | | | | | | |
| T= | | | | | | | | | | | |

## Individual student observation

| Time | Student behaviour | Apparent cause |
| --- | --- | --- |
|  |  |  |
|  |  |  |
|  |  |  |
|  |  |  |
|  |  |  |
|  |  |  |
|  |  |  |
|  |  |  |
|  |  |  |
|  |  |  |
|  |  |  |
|  |  |  |
|  |  |  |
|  |  |  |
|  |  |  |
|  |  |  |
|  |  |  |
|  |  |  |
|  |  |  |
|  |  |  |
|  |  |  |
|  |  |  |

## How to Succeed as an Elementary Teacher

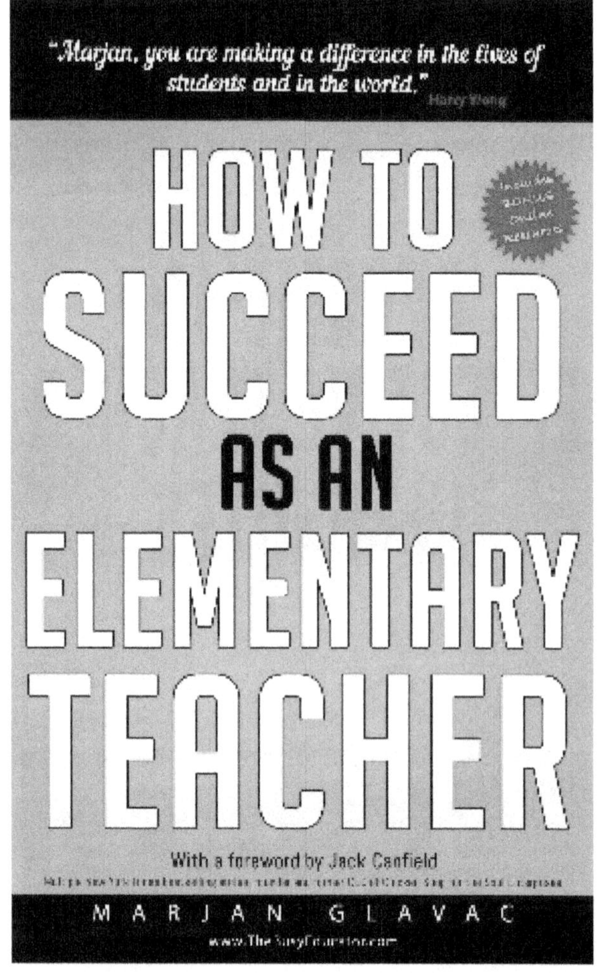

## Teaching Is... Moments that inspire and Motivate Teachers to Make a Difference

One more thing…

Enjoyed This Book?

You Can Make A Difference

Thank you very much for purchasing this book *How to Thrive and Survive in Your Classroom*. We're very grateful that you chose this book from all the other wonderful books on the market.

I hope this book made your life as an elementary teacher that much more enjoyable for you and your students. If it did, please consider sharing your thoughts with your fellow teachers on Facebook, Twitter, LinkedIn and Instagram.

If you enjoyed this book and found value in reading it, please take few minutes to post an honest review for the book. Reviews are very important to readers and authors—and difficult to get. Reviews don't have to be long: even a sentence or two is a huge help. Every review helps.

While on your favorite review site, feel free to vote for helpful reviews. The top-voted reviews are featured for display, and most likely to influence new readers. You can vote for as many reviews as you like.

All the best,

Paul Jackson and Marjan Glavac

Printed in Great Britain
by Amazon

57737807R00111